The Transfer Student's Guide to the College Experience

Nadine S. Koch
California State University, Los Angeles

K. William Wasson
California State University, Los Angeles

Houghton Mifflin Company
Boston   New York

To my wonderful family and loving husband, Hal   N. S. K.

To my parents, Lula and William G.   K. W. W.

Director of College Survival: Barbara A. Heinssen
Assistant Editor: Shani B. Fisher
Associate Project Editor: Kate Hartke
Editorial Assistant: Shanya Dingle
Senior Production/Design Coordinator: Carol Merrigan
Senior Manufacturing Coordinator: Jane Spelman
Marketing Manager: Barbara LeBuhn

Cover Image: Eyewire

Acknowledgments
p. 69: Carol Kanar, *The Confident Student,* Fourth Edition. Copyright © 2001 by Houghton
Mifflin Company. Reprinted with permission; p. 69: Reprinted with permission from David Ellis,
Becoming a Master Student, Ninth Edition. Copyright © 2001 by Houghton Mifflin Company.
Reprinted with permission; p. 75: Regina Hellyer, Carol Robinson, and Phyllis Sherwood, *Study
Skills for Learning Power,* Second Edition. Copyright © 2001 by Houghton Mifflin Company.
Reprinted with permission; p. 85: *Symbolic Interactionism,* Sixth Edition, by Joel Charon. Copy-
right © 1998. Reprinted by permission of Pearson Education, Inc., Upper Saddle River, NJ
07458; p. 99: Copyright © 1998 by Houghton Mifflin Company. Reproduced by permission
from *Compact American Dictionary;* p. 100: Reprinted by permission of the author from Donald
Urquidi, *Decoding Media Messages II,* Second Edition; p. 130: Gerald Schiffhorst and David
Pharr, *The Short Handbook for Writers,* Second Edition. Copyright © 1982 Scott Foresman and
Company. Reprinted by permission of The McGraw-Hill Companies; p.150: Portions of Chapter
9 discussing the products of Personal Strengths Publishing, specifically the Personal Values Inven-
tory®, Strength Deployment Inventory® Facilitation Guide and Relationship Awareness® Theory
Manual of Administration and Interpretation, 9th Edition are presented through the courtesy of
Mr. Tim Scudder, CEO, Personal Strengths Publishing, P. O. Box 2605, Carlsbad, CA 92018-
2605 or *www.personalstrengths.com;* p. 184: Copyright © 2001 Bankrate.com. Reprinted with
permission.

Printed in the U.S.A.
Library of Congress Control Number: 2001092100

ISBN: 0-618-07716-2

123456789-BBS-05 04 03 02 01

As part of Houghton Mifflin's ongoing
commitment to the environment, this
text has been printed on recycled paper.

CONTENTS

Many interesting things happen to us in life that are unplanned. This book is the end result of one of those unplanned events. While we had intended to look exclusively at the dropout rates of entering first-year students at California State University, Los Angeles, we stumbled upon some unanticipated and rather disturbing additional data: transfer students were dropping out during their first year at about the same rate as freshmen. We thought that this information couldn't possibly be accurate. It seemed obvious that transfer students had already proven themselves to be successful college students. They had survived one or two years of college before transferring to our institution. Something was terribly wrong. What challenges were causing transfer students to drop out at rates approaching those of entering freshmen? Was this problem unique to our particular institution or were other campuses experiencing the same problem? Most important, we wanted to discover how we could help transfer students to succeed and graduate.

Once we started researching the problem, we found the experiences of transfer students on our campus to be fairly typical of transfer students nationwide. There is a broad range of issues facing transfer students during their first year at their new institution. Financial, academic, physical, and psychological pressures affect transfer students; if left unaddressed, these concerns can undermine their success.

At our university, we recognized that we had a problem and quickly instituted a mandatory transfer student course to help students adjust to the university and to provide them with the necessary skills and resources to successfully fulfill their academic dreams. This book was born out of our experiences of talking to, teaching, and listening to our transfer students.

The Transfer Student's Guide to the College Experience is not a philosophical textbook but is designed to provide sound and practical advice. The book is divided into three distinct parts. Part I, "Your New University," will help you to navigate your new surroundings. It will demystify the organization of your new academic institution and will give you a map to successfully use university rules and procedures to your best advantage. The first three chapters are organized around a series of frequently asked questions (FAQs).

Part II, "Strategies for Academic Success," will provide you with academic and life-management skills. These chapters focus on academic requirements and expectations as you advance to the upper division level. You will learn how to take notes, manage your time, study more effectively, think critically, take exams, and write papers.

Part III, "Planning for Life During College and Beyond," helps you determine the direction of your life by investigating your particular values, goals, and motivations. The focus is on aligning your educational, professional, and career goals with your personal values, likes, and dislikes. You will learn how to manage your money and plan for life after college.

Special Features of this Book

- **Frequently Asked Questions (FAQs)** are the organizational feature of the chapters in Part I, addressing major concerns of students transferring to a new institution.

- Numerous **interactive exercises** connect you with your campus community and help you discover its physical aspects, student body, faculty and staff, and technology. Exercises designed to assist in your academic and personal development have you engage in activities that are directly applicable to your coursework.

- **Computer exercises**, within each chapter, will acquaint you with your campus technology and explain how to responsibly use Internet technology.

- Our **website** contains additional activities, health tips, and references. Visit **http://college.hmco.com**.

- An **instructor's manual** offers specific suggestions for classroom presentations and activities.

- **College Survival Consulting Services**—College Survival is the leading source of expertise, support services, and materials for student success courses. We are committed to promoting and supporting effective success courses within the higher education community.

  For more than fifteen years, Houghton Mifflin's College Survival consultants have provided consultation and training for the design, implementation, and presentation of student success and first-year courses. Our team of consultants have a wide variety of experience in teaching and administering the first-year course. We can provide help in establishing or improving your student success program. We offer assistance in course design, instructor training, teaching strategies, and much more. Contact us today at 1-800-528-8323, or visit us on the web at **college.hmco.com**.

- The **Myers-Briggs Type Indicator® (MBTI®) Instrument** is the most widely used personality inventory in history—and it is available as a shrink wrap with *The Transfer Student's Guide to the College Experience* for a discounted price at qualified schools. The standard form M self-scorable instrument contains 93 items that determine preferences on four scales: Extraversion-Introversion, Sensing-Intuition, Thinking-Feeling, and Judging-

Perceiving. (MBTI and Myers-Briggs Type Indicator are registered trademarks of Consulting Psychologists Press, Inc.)

- Also available for shrink wrap is the **Retention Management System™ College Student Inventory** from Noel Levitz. As a specially priced package, this early-alert, early-intervention program identifies students with tendencies that contribute to dropping out of school. Students can participate in an integrated, campus-wide program. Advisors are sent three interpretative reports: The Student's Report, the Advisor/Counselor Report, and The College Summary and Planning Report. For more information, contact your College Survival consultant at 1-800-528-8323 or your local Houghton Mifflin Sales Representative.

- **The College Survival Student Planner** is a week-at-a-glance academic planner, available in a specially priced package with this text. Produced in partnership with Premier, A Franklin Covey Company, The College Survival Student Planner assists students in managing their time on—and off—campus. The planner includes a "Survival Kit" of helpful success tips from Houghton Mifflin Company College Survival textbooks.

Acknowledgments

There were many people without whose help this book would not exist. First, we offer our thanks to our Houghton Mifflin book representative, Gina Montoya, who heard about our work with transfer students and presented us with the idea of writing this textbook. In addition to Gina, we offer heartfelt thanks to Barbara Heinssen, director of College Survival at Houghton Mifflin, for her enthusiasm and unwavering support. Thanks also to editorial assistants Shani Fisher and Jonathan Wolf, who were quick to respond to our every question and concern. And a very special thanks to Kate Hartke whose patience and keen eye were much appreciated. To the College Survival team of Sandi Ayaz, Derek Jeske, and Julio Trujillo, thank you for your kind support and efforts on behalf of this book.

A number of reviewers have made valuable contributions to this book, and we would like to thank them for their guidance:

Becky Boesch, Portland State University, OR

Mona J. Casady, Southwest Missouri State University, MO

Kara Craig, University of Southern Mississippi, MS

Viki Sox Fecas, University of South Carolina, SC

Frank Gelin, British Columbia Council on Admissions and Transfer

Barbara J. Goldberg, University of Maryland, MD

Manuel N. Gómez, University of California, Irvine, CA

Beverly Greenfeig, University of Maryland, MD

Jacqueline Groot, SUNY Cortland, NY

Russell Haynes, Odessa College, TX

Teri Hollander, University System of Maryland Headquarters, MD

Kathryn Jones, University of California, Riverside, CA

Gene L. Newman, The University of Louisiana at Monroe, LA

Pamela Isacco Niesslein, College of Charleston, SC

Mark L. Allen Poisel, University of Central Florida, FL

Elva Short, Texas A&M University-Kingsville, TX

Barbara K. Wade, Pennsylvania State University, PA

We would also like to specifically thank two of our student reviewers, Maricel Baclit and Daniel Quesada.

At California State University, Los Angeles, we would like to express our deep appreciation to our colleagues, who are committed to student success and recognized early on the special challenges facing transfer students. We wish we could name all of them but they are too numerous to mention. We want to specifically thank Alfredo Gonzalez, Dean of Undergraduate Studies, who deserves special acknowledgment for his institutional support of programs assisting transfer students and particularly for his enthusiasm and support of this book.

On a personal note, we wish to thank our friends and families, who patiently (and sometimes *very* patiently) understood the demands involved in writing this book and the necessity for our many declined invitations and incommunicative hours. A special heartfelt thanks to Hal Steinberg, husband extraordinaire, for his support and assistance (an unanticipated benefit to him was the extra alone time to improve his golf game). Finally, we wish to thank each other as co-authors. Although we come from different academic disciplines (political science and sociology), we worked very well together due to our philosophical and practical knowledge and experiences in this field and our commitment to student success.

N. S. K.
K. W. W.

CHAPTER 1

Transitions: Charting a New Course

WARNING: Transferring may be hazardous to your academic health and has been associated with higher rates of dropping out! However, using this book may minimize the dangers and maximize your potential.

As a transfer student, you already have proven yourself to be a successful college student. You have attended college, and may have earned an A.A. degree. You've done well enough to transfer to a four-year institution.

Even so, researchers have reported dropout rates among transfer students to be unexpectedly high. Some estimate that 15–20% of all transfer students drop out sometime during the first year at their new institution. Other researchers have found that transfer students experience a decline in their grade point average (GPA) during their initial term of enrollment at a four-year institution.

These statistics are daunting. Transfer students are "survivors" who have already completed one or even two years of college. Yet something happens in the transition to the four-year institution that causes some transfer students to drop out during their first year and/or to experience a decline in academic performance during their first term. The purpose of this book is to prepare you, the transfer student, for success at a four-year institution. We believe that with the proper skills, attitudes, and knowledge you can successfully achieve your academic goals.

FAQ: I'm not a freshman. I've attended college for a couple of years and did well enough to transfer to the university. Why should I worry about the transition to my new four-year institution?

TRANSFER SHOCK

Transfer shock is the term that refers to all the changes that occur in your life when you transfer from one college—usually a community college or smaller institution—to a university. You may experience changes in your academic life, your physical state, and your state of mind, as well as your environment. In this section, we have listed the ten major differences that probably exist between your previous college and the one you are now attending. The list describes some of the most important changes involved in transferring to a university. This book will provide practical solutions and skills that will help you to minimize the impact of these challenges. And we will provide you with tools and information you can use to maximize your chances of having a successful university experience as a transfer student and of actually enjoying this special time in your life.

Differences Between Your Previous School and Your Four-Year University

1. **Larger school.** Most students transfer from a smaller college to a larger university, so your new campus is probably much larger in both area and student enrollment. You might find it more difficult to navigate in a physical sense and in a social sense as well.

2. **Larger classes.** There usually are more students enrolled at the university, and classes are usually larger. You might even find yourself in a large lecture course. These larger lecture halls can accommodate 150–500 students per class!

3. **Televised/video/Internet courses.** Welcome to the technology age. Many universities offer courses taught via the Internet (called Distance Learning because students are some distance from campus, usually at home, when they interact with the course materials). Some institutions also offer televised or videotaped courses. Videos of the professor's lectures are played in class, and teaching assistants are present to answer questions.

4. **Impersonal atmosphere.** Because of its size and larger student population, your new campus will probably seem less personal. Being new to this environment, you may at first experience feelings of isolation and loneliness.

5. **Financial pressures.** Education costs are typically greater at a four-year university than at a community college. Students may experience more than a four-fold increase in tuition as they go from a community college to a public university. Financial aid, scholarships, and grants don't always meet these increased expenses. Many students need to work to cover them. Work puts an additional burden on the student, diverting time from studies and college life in general.

6. **Academic advisement.** Although there are more class choices at the university and you have more freedom in selecting courses you want to take, there is less advice. It becomes the student's responsibility to seek academic advice. Very little hand-holding goes on at the university level. Unfortunately, many students see an advisor late in the game, only to find out that they've taken courses they didn't need and neglected to take courses they did need in order to graduate. The cost of this delay, in terms of time and money, can

be very high. More time may have to be spent in college to meet the requirements to graduate.

7. **Different academic standards and requirements.** The coursework and requirements of a four-year university are sometimes more difficult than those at a two-year institution. In addition, if you finished your lower-division general-education courses before you transferred, you are now ready to enroll in upper-division classes. Upper-division courses are intellectually more demanding, and professors expect more from upper-division students. You may be at a disadvantage when compared to other students who have already studied in the university setting—and who may even have had some of the same professors in their lower-division classes.

8. **Different expectations.** You need to become acclimated quickly to the university environment with its new demands and standards. Your academic and personal performance will be judged according to the standards of your new institution. You must make sure you understand all of the rules, policies, regulations, and norms (unwritten rules of behavior) of your new school.

9. **Time management.** There is more coursework, more studying, higher costs, and (for some) more outside work hours. How are you going to manage these increased demands on your time? It becomes critical for the university student to develop time management skills. This is not a philosophical issue; it is a matter of survival.

10. **Personal issues.** As each person matures, life's personal issues usually become more complex and demanding. During your time at the university, most of you will have personal life issues that will need to be dealt with. It is important to learn to minimize the negative influence of these pressures on your academic life.

E X E R C I S E   1.1

TRANSFER SHOCK

For each of these ten major challenges related to transferring, write one or two sentences describing your experience with these changes since transferring to your new institution.

1. Larger school _____

_____

_____

2. Larger classes _____

_____

_____

3. Televised/video/Internet courses _____

_____

_____

4. Impersonal atmosphere _____

_____

_____

5. Financial pressures _____

_____

_____

6. Academic advisement _____

_____

_____

7. Different academic standards and requirements _____

_____

_____

8. Different expectations _____

_____

_____

9. Time management _____

_____

_____

10. Personal issues _____

_____

_____

FAQ: Aren't all colleges basically the same? How could my new university be so different from the campus I've transferred from? And what possible impact could it have on me?

BASIC FACTS ABOUT INSTITUTIONS OF HIGHER LEARNING

There are differences among institutions of higher learning, and it is important that you understand what *type* of institution you are now attending. It is also important to understand where you came from (no, this is not a lesson about "the birds and the bees"). That is, you need to know what type of institution you just transferred from. Different types of institutions offer a variety of resources, emphasize different things, have different "missions," vary in educational philosophy, and may differ in appearance and organization. In the paragraphs that follow, we briefly describe several types of academic institutions. You should recognize your current institution, as well as the institution you were attending before you transferred.

Community Colleges

Community colleges are also known as two-year colleges or junior colleges. Nearly one-third of all community college students transfer to a four-year college. Community colleges confer a diploma known as an Associates Degree. It indicates that two years of college-level work have been completed. Many transfer students enter the four-year college with General Education Certification, which is the official notice of completion of G.E. at the community college level. Few, if any, advanced courses (upper-division college courses) are offered at the community college level.

Technical Colleges

Technical colleges are generally two-year colleges, although some offer four-year technical programs. The two-year technical colleges offer Associates Degrees in a variety of technical career fields. Technical colleges can specialize in fields such as biotechnology, nursing, automotive technology, design, architecture, manufacturing, and computer technology, to name a few. The types of courses and programs available vary greatly from college to college.

Liberal Arts Colleges

Liberal arts colleges focus almost exclusively on undergraduate education—that is, they do not offer graduate degrees. Most liberal arts colleges are private, receiving most of their funding from various private sources. The curriculum at liberal arts colleges concentrates on the humanities: literature, history, the arts, and philosophy.

Universities

The **university** is the institution that offers the widest range of academic programs. Many universities, public and private, have graduate students enrolled in Master's and Ph.D. programs. A Master's Degree usually requires at least 45 quarter-units of additional course work, mostly at the graduate level, after completion of a Bachelor's Degree. Earning a doctorate (Ph.D.) requires a greater amount of graduate work. If you are attending a university, you may share some of your advanced upper-division classes with graduate students. They are sometimes allowed to take important undergraduate courses as prerequisites for their graduate program. Don't be confused or alarmed if you hear them talking about course or program requirements different from yours. They are following a different program.

Teaching Versus Research Institutions

Institutions can be further classified in terms of the amount of teaching and research expected of the faculty. **Teaching institutions** are colleges and universities where faculty members primarily teach. Typically, there are no or few Ph.D. programs and few Master's programs. The faculty spend most of their time teaching. Many professors conduct research but in a limited manner.

At **research universities**, faculty members teach but are also heavily engaged in research. Most research institutions offer Master's and Ph.D. degrees. At research universities, faculty members often have grants from the government or other public or private organizations to conduct extensive research on specific topics. A substantial portion of the faculty members' time is thus devoted to research.

FAQ: My professor is always talking about her research. It is really interesting, and I would love to learn more about it and maybe even help with the study. Is it okay to talk to my professor about this?

If you are interested in research, by all means talk to your professor about your interests. Most professors love to talk about their research, and many are often looking for students who are interested in participating in the research process. Sometimes this may even be in a paid capacity. You can *earn while you learn*.

EXERCISE 1.2

INSTITUTIONS OF HIGHER LEARNING

Identify the type of institution you attended before transferring. What type of institution are you now attending?

a. Type of institution transferred from: _____

b. Type of institution now attending: _____

List three things you learned about your current institution from this chapter:

1. _____

_____

2. _____

_____

3. _____

_____

FAQ: There are many more students at my new campus. Who are all these people?

DIFFERENT TYPES OF STUDENTS

Contrary to popular opinion—and contrary to the way television stereotypes college life—there is no "typical" college student. College students are a very diverse group of people.

Traditional Versus Nontraditional Students

Traditional students are those who are young (18–22 years of age), single, and childless; are enrolled full-time; and generally do not work while attending

Bob Daemmrich/The Image Works

college. Students who don't fit this stereotypical profile are usually referred to as **nontraditional students**. Because of the numerous demands on nontraditional students' time, many don't complete their Bachelor's Degree in four years. Because traditional students generally have fewer responsibilities and attend college full-time, they can usually earn their Bachelor's Degree in four years. The number of today's college students classified as nontraditional is growing larger each year.

Younger Versus "Older" Students

The stereotype of college students ranging in age from 18 to 22 is no longer valid. Students span the entire age spectrum. Believe it or not, some campuses (usually universities in urban areas) admit students as young as 10 years old into special programs for the very young, very academically gifted. Other campuses are home to students in their sixties and seventies. Older students can add a unique dimension to the learning experience. Having worked and raised families, they can draw upon these life experiences to offer a different perspective in class discussions. Many times it is the older students who liven up a class.

For those older students who quit college many years ago and are now returning to resume their studies, the adjustment can be quite demanding. More campuses are beginning to recognize the obstacles that older, returning students face and are creating unique services to ease their transition back to campus life.

Full-time Versus Part-time Students

Your campus probably hosts both full-time and part-time students. If you are attending a small, liberal arts college, most of your classmates may be full-time traditional students. At larger, public institutions you may find equal numbers of full-time and part-time students.

Each institution has rules stating how many units or courses you must enroll in to be considered full-time. This is an important piece of information. Scholarships, grants, and financial aid are often tied to your enrollment status. Full-time enrollment is usually required to qualify for disbursement of funds. If you register for enough courses to meet the requirements for full-time status and then drop a course or two, this may mean you've assumed part-time status. Check the rules, and keep track of how many units/courses you are officially enrolled in.

 FAQ: My classmate told me he is a returning student. What does it mean to be a returning student? Why is this designation important?

Continuous Versus Returning Students

This is a very important distinction. A **continuous student** is someone who has started college and has remained enrolled without dropping out for any extended period of time. The definition of allowable time away from school varies from school to school. It is imperative that you determine the exact definition used by the institution you attend. Some institutions allow you to skip *one* term, others more, and still others less. You need to consult your advisor or college catalog for the rules pertaining to your school. By the way, not attending summer session is okay. You still get to keep your status as a continuous student. Everyone needs a break for *fun in the sun* (or gainful employment—a change can be as good as a rest).

Why is knowing your enrollment status so important? If you break your continuous enrollment and are classified as a returning student, you will probably be subject to a different set of requirements for graduation. Let's say you started college, attended for two years, and then took a break. Then, after three years away from school, you decide you want to resume your college studies (a very wise choice, indeed). You will be required to reapply for admission, and once readmitted, you will be classified as a **returning student**. The big deal here is that you probably are now subject to the college requirements in effect at the time of your readmittance, not the requirements that existed at the time of your original attendance. Starting to see what's happening here? You entered into the university under one set of requirements and designed your sequence of classes accordingly. Now, three years later, the rules of the game may have changed. You may be required to take all the current requirements, and some of your prior classes may no longer fulfill these requirements. Remember, by leaving the institution for a prolonged period of time, you forfeit your continuous student status. **Be extremely careful to avoid this potential danger.**

 FAQ: I've always been a commuter student. How do the experiences of commuter students differ from those of students who live on campus?

Commuter Versus Residential Schools

Some institutions are **residential schools**; most students live on campus. Other colleges are considered **commuter schools** because the student body commutes from home to school. Residential colleges are different from commuter colleges. There is a difference in atmosphere and in the programs and activities offered to students. The first thing you notice when you are living on campus is that there are always other students around. Libraries usually stay open late (at some schools they are open 24/7), and there are places for late-night eating. At residential institutions, enjoyable extracurricular activities and events are regularly scheduled on campus and in housing complexes.

Students who attend commuter schools generally spend less time on campus. Commuter students come to campus for their specific classes at specified times. Once classes are over, these students usually leave campus. This does not mean that commuter schools don't have any extracurricular activities. In fact, they have many. It's just that the nature of the student population means that the students tend not to participate in such numbers as students at residential colleges.

One of the disadvantages of being a commuter student is that one may not take the time to explore the campus to find out about exciting upcoming events. Many do not realize that there is life to the campus outside the classrooms. If you are a commuter student, try to spend some time just hanging out on campus and take advantage of some planned activities. The Student Union or Campus Center building usually has information on all campus events. Also, check with your major department for any clubs or organizations you may join.

Working Versus Nonworking Students

Many students need to work while attending college. At larger four-year colleges, many of the students work, some even holding full-time jobs. Obviously, the more time a student spends at work, the less time he or she will have to devote to classes and other college activities. It has been estimated that for every *one* hour a student spends in class, the student needs to allocate, on average, about *two* hours of study time. Some courses may require less study time, others more. Using this formula, you can see how difficult it is to balance work, classes, and studying, not to mention time for leisure, recreation, sleep, eating, commuting, and other activities. But we will leave this for the chapter on time management.

Work often detracts from the college experience, and one should work the least amount of time possible. Once you graduate and enter the work force, you will have many years (decades!) of work. You have only one chance to be an undergraduate student and to enjoy campus life.

The Student as Parent: Dual Responsibilities

Because there are many "older" students attending college, it is not surprising that some college students also have parenting responsibilities. Does being a parent *and* attending college present special challenges? Absolutely. Parents have additional responsibilities and major time commitments related to family life. (And think of the single parent! All child-rearing responsibilities fall on the shoulders of that one person.) Add to parenting responsibilities the fact that many students with children have to work to support their families. This is a triple burden: school, work, and children. Many campuses, especially those where substantial numbers of parents are enrolled, offer workshops and support groups focusing on issues important to students raising children. And a number of campuses have on-site, affordable day care centers staffed by students preparing to become teachers. If you are a parent, check with your college to see what assistance and resources are available.

FAQ: I am a single parent caring for two children. I would like to carry a full academic load. What issues should I be concerned about in balancing these two important roles?

Like working students, parents often have trouble managing their time, squeeze too much into their days, and fail to have a backup system in place. Problems with your child are not always valid excuses for missing class, turning assignments in late, or failing to appear for important exams or presentations. Some professors are not sympathetic to cries for leniency because a child became ill or the babysitter didn't show up. If you have parenting responsibilities, you must have a backup plan. Enlist the help of family members, friends, and neighbors who can provide child care so that you can attend class. It sounds cold-hearted, but professors insist that school be your number-one priority. You may have to reduce your course load if family responsibilities demand too much of your time and attention. Better yet, plan carefully and realistically when you schedule your classes.

FAQ: The other day someone asked me what "school" I was in. I had no idea what they meant! I know my major department but nothing more than that. How is the university organized?

ORGANIZATIONAL STRUCTURE OF COLLEGES AND UNIVERSITIES

There is a general organizational structure to universities, though some variations always will exist. Figure 1.1 outlines the basic structure of a university.

Key Terms in the Organizational Hierarchy

University is the term used to describe the entire institution. It includes all the colleges, schools, divisions, and departments. Your university might be part of a state university system, such as the California State University (CSU) system, the State University of New York (SUNY) system, or the University of Texas (UT) system. The individual responsible for the entire system is usually called the **chancellor**. The **president** is the chief officer of a particular university. The **provost** is second in command, reporting directly to the president. Some universities have what are known as **colleges** as the major educational units in their structure. These colleges are specialized parts of the university, such as the College of Law, College of Veterinary Medicine, College of Dentistry, and College of Liberal Arts. Other universities have **schools** as their larger educational units. Like colleges, these schools are specialized educational units, such as the School of Medicine, School of Natural and Social Sciences, and School of Arts and Letters. And some universities have **divisions** as their major educational units. Universities are generally organized into colleges, schools, divisions, or some combination of the three. Again, many variations exist. **Deans** head schools and colleges. The person in charge of a division is usually called the division **director**. The smallest unit in the university is the **department**. Departments usually focus on a particular discipline; examples include the Political Science Department, Business Administration Department, Psychology Department, Chemistry Department, and English Department. **Chairs** head departments.

Your Place in the Organizational Structure

Now, to the specifics of your major and how the organizational structure affects you personally. The major you have selected is part of a department. That department is one of many departments in a division, school, or college. That division, school, or college, along with many others, makes up the university. Got it? It can be confusing, but it is important to know to which division, school, or college you belong. To find out, consult your university catalog or ask the secretary in your major department. Sometimes divisions, schools, and colleges offer special programs to their students and may even have scholarship money available to students majoring in their departments. Additionally, you

EXERCISE 1.3

STUDENT PROFILE

In this section, we reviewed the different types of students attending universities. For each category listed below, briefly describe *your* situation, indicating how it will affect your university experience.

a. Traditional or nontraditional student? _____

_____

_____

b. Younger or older student?_____

_____

_____

c. Full-time or part-time student? _____

_____

_____

d. Continuing or returning student?_____

_____

_____

e. Commuter or residential student? _____

_____

_____

f. Working or nonworking student?_____

_____

_____

g. Parent or not a parent? _____

_____

_____

may have to visit your division director or your college/school dean to get his or her signature on a form to add or drop a course. It is important to know which division, school, or college you belong to; where that office is located; and, if you are really ambitious, the director or dean's name.

 FAQ: I haven't yet declared a major. Where do I fit in the university structure?

Undeclared Majors

If you have not yet selected a major, you will need to find the office that deals with undeclared majors. Consult your campus directory or ask any advisor or professor. Forms requiring the signature of the department chair will need to be signed by the appropriate person who is responsible for undeclared majors. This is another reason why it is wise to select and declare your major as early as possible.

 FAQ: Some of my professors are instructors, others are assistant professors, and I have one class taught by a T.A. What are the differences among these different titles?

Figure 1.1

Organizational structure of universities

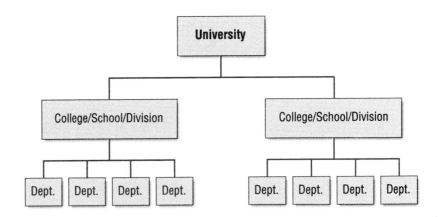

E X E R C I S E 1.4

ORGANIZATIONAL STRUCTURE

The purpose of this exercise is for you to become acquainted with the organizational structure of your university. The information you will collect is important to your college experience. You will be able to see how and where you fit into the organization.

a. Is your university part of a larger university system? If so, which one? What is the chancellor's name? _____

_____

b. Find out the name of the president of your university and where his or her office is located. _____

_____

c. For your major department, or the discipline you are considering majoring in, find out the name of the college, school, or division it is in. Who is the dean or director? Where is that person's office located? (If you have not declared a major, then indicate where and from whom undeclared majors obtain assistance.) _____

_____

d. Who is the chair of your major department? Where is the department located? Where is the chair's office located? (For those who have not declared a major, find the appropriate information.)_____

_____

e. Where is your advisor's office? Telephone number? Name of advisor?_____

_____

f. Who is the secretary in your major department (or office for those who have not declared a major)? What is his or her telephone number? _____

_____

g. List the sources you used to gather this information. _____

_____

_____

_____

UNIVERSITY FACULTY

Those teaching you will have a specified professional designation, or *rank*. Here is a brief description of the various ranks, moving from the lowest to the highest.

Faculty Ranks

Graduate Teaching Assistants

T.A.s typically are graduate students pursuing an advanced degree (usually a Ph.D.) at the university. You may have a graduate student teaching a course or assisting your professor in some other capacity. At larger universities, where hundreds of students are assigned to one class, a professor will need the assistance of one or even more graduate students. These graduate teaching assistants usually have office hours during which you can meet with them to review the class lectures and assignments.

Instructor

Teaching faculty who are not permanent members of the university faculty are often given the title of instructor. Some instructors have Ph.D.s (doctorates); others do not. Instructors can be hired on a full-time basis, or they can serve as part-time faculty.

Assistant Professor

Faculty usually start at this level and begin to work their way up the ranks. Assistant professors have little seniority and usually spend six years at this level until they have gained enough experience—and have accomplished enough professionally—to be promoted to the associate level.

Associate Professor

Associate professors have some seniority. Most professors are promoted to this mid-level position when they are granted tenure. Again, each university sets its own standards for promotion to the rank of associate.

Full Professor

Faculty with the most seniority and accomplishments advance to this level, which is generally the highest faculty rank.

FAQ: What is tenure? (Or, why does my professor seem so nervous?)

Tenure

Being granted tenure is important to your professor, and you need to understand what it is. Many faculty are hired for what is called a tenure-track position. This means that the department that hired the faculty member hopes to keep him or her at the university on a permanent basis. The professor is usually hired at an assistant professor rank and has approximately six years to prove to his or her professional colleagues, and to the university at large, that he or she is a valuable member of the academic community and deserving of tenure. If tenure is awarded, the faculty member can remain at the university indefinitely. In addition, tenure usually brings a promotion to associate professor. If tenure is denied, the person has to leave the university at the end of the following year (yes, it is similar to being fired). This is why faculty get very nervous around the time they are being reviewed for tenure. It is a very difficult, tension-filled period.

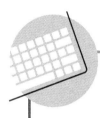

C O M P U T E R   E X E R C I S E   1.5

VISITING YOUR UNIVERSITY'S WEB SITE

Most universities have an Internet web site. Find your institution's web site. If you don't know the address, call one of the campus computer centers for the information.

a. Write down your university's web site address: _____

_____

b. List the major features offered on the home page of your university's web site. _____

_____

_____

_____

c. Describe three things you learned from your university's web site. _____

_____

_____

_____

d. If links to other web sites are available, link to one of them and describe what you find at the linked site. _____

_____

_____

_____

COMPUTER EXERCISE 1.6

EMAILING A PROFESSOR

In order to complete this exercise, you must have a campus computer account or the ability to email from home to campus.

a. You are to email one of your professors a brief message. Many professors include an email address on their course syllabi. If you do not have email addresses for any of your professors, you need to ask at least one of your professors for his or her email address.

b. Email your professor with a question about the class material, an assignment, the campus, or his or her professional life. Here's an example of an appropriate message:

Dear Professor Jones,

I am enjoying your course on cultural anthropology. I am considering a major in this area. Could I make an appointment to meet with you to discuss some career options? When would be the best time to meet, and where should I meet you?

Thank you,

Mary Smith, a student in your Anthro 250 course

c. Print out a copy of the message you sent and a copy of the message you received in response. Attach these to the sheet you turn in with this assignment.

CHAPTER 2

Learning About the University's Rules and Policies

SOURCES OF INFORMATION

If you were to arrive in a city in another country, you would find a road map of the area to navigate in unfamiliar territory and learn the "rules of the road." Similarly, you will need to learn your way around your university campus, procedurally as well as geographically! Students entering a new university may get information on rules and policies from several different sources.

University Web Site

Log onto the university's web site on the Internet, if available, and open the appropriate web page for the information you seek. Many times, the university will have an Advisement Bulletin Board that answers frequently asked questions and includes an interactive component that lets you state your question to a member of the university's academic advisement center. The center will respond promptly. *Note:* During the enrollment process, you should have received instructions on how to use the university's computerized information systems, which may include your own personal "username" and "password."

University Catalog

Obtain a copy of the general catalog of your university. It will contain all the rules and regulations about personal behavior, information on all university programs and degree options, and the location of support offices or programs. This general catalog is, in effect, a contract between you and the university. It specifies the academic requirements you must complete to earn a degree from this school.

Schedule of Classes

Obtain a copy of the "Schedule of Classes" or its equivalent for the academic period (quarter or semester) of your entrance. This will contain

- Information on how to register for classes
- Up-to-date information on course offerings
- Current-quarter/semester and future course offerings
- Important dates in this academic period, such as the last day on which you may add or drop a class, how far into the academic term tuition refunds are possible, emergency withdrawals, and dates and times of final examinations
- Any policy or procedure change made since the last printing of the general catalog

Student Handbook

Many campuses provide a student handbook or student survival guide for entering students. It has current and insightful information. These handbooks are generally available through the orientation office, at the admissions or registration offices, and at the campus bookstore. Even if you have to buy it, this is a worthwhile item to purchase.

Academic Advisor

Schedule an appointment with your academic advisor—that is, the advisor for your major at your four-year school. If your major is undecided or undeclared, then make an appointment with the university's academic advisement center. Your academic advisor will be a key individual throughout your career at this campus. It is important to meet and work with her or him early, during the first academic term at your new university.

Remember to ask about your graduation check. On many campuses, you must begin the process of having the formal evaluation for your graduation up to one year before your scheduled graduation date.

Counselors and Advisors

 FAQ: Why should I see an advisor? I saw my college counselor before I transferred.

Advisement is an ongoing process whatever school you attend. There are differences between university advisors or community college counselors and between the types of information they provide. In addition, some universities provide an electronic Advisement Bulletin Board to answer frequently asked questions.

EXERCISE 2.1

GENERAL CATALOG

Using your general catalog, locate the following pieces of information. Then write, for your own use, a brief notation and the page number or Internet address where you located this information.

Student Services and Activities

How many scholarships are available in your major on this campus? What are they? ___

_____

_____

How many general scholarships are available on this campus? What are they?_____

_____

_____

Where can students with a physical or learning disability go for assistance on this campus? What kind of assistance can they expect?_____

_____

_____

How many social fraternities and sororities offer membership on this campus? What are they? _____

_____

_____

How many academic clubs or organizations related to your major are there on campus? How can you become a member?_____

_____

_____

How and where do you register or sign up for required university tests? _____

_____

_____

When do you apply for graduation? That is, how many academic terms or units must you complete before applying for graduation? (You fill out forms indicating what name you want on your diploma, and you generally receive tickets for your family members to attend the graduation ceremony.) Where do you apply?_____

_____

_____

What kind of honors programs are available on campus? Where do you apply? _____

_____

_____

What are the types and locations of writing and tutorial assistance on campus? _____

_____

_____

In how many countries may you attend "sister" universities and receive credit at this university? What are these institutions? _____

_____

_____

Consider also whether you can answer the following questions:

What about the campus honor code?

What does the term *academic honesty* mean?

What do *plagiarism* and *cheating* mean?

What are the rules for living with other students in university housing?

What can I do if I feel I am being discriminated against?

Where can I go if I am being harassed sexually, physically, or emotionally?

What rules govern student–teacher relationships?

All of the answers to these questions can be found in your general catalog.

Community college **counselors** may be of several types, including college counselors, career counselors, and psychological counselors. We will discuss the college counselor who gives general guidance about

1. The requirements for transfer to a four-year university.
2. The lists of the majors and minors you may consider or declare at your new campus.
3. Any forms and petitions you may need to apply.

Advisors, on the other hand, are oriented toward academic goals. Each transfer student should set up an appointment with the academic advisor for her or his major, if declared, or with the university's academic advisement center, to receive

1. A specific program of study for the major and minor, including required courses and recommended courses.

E X E R C I S E *2.2*

SCHEDULE OF CLASSES

Using your "Schedule of Classes," locate the following pieces of information and write, for your use, a brief notation and the number of the page on which you located that information.

Using This Schedule

How do I read this book? How is it organized? _____

_____

What is considered a "normal" study load here? That is, how many class units do students usually carry? _____

_____

How many weeks of class are there in the academic periods at this university? _____

_____

Where do I find information on how to enroll by telephone or via the Internet? _____

_____

How do I find information in the Schedule of Classes to plan my courses three academic periods into the future? _____

_____

Where do I find information on where to go for financial aid? _____

_____

Where do I go for tutorial help? _____

_____

Where do I go for writing assistance? _____

Where is the final exam schedule? _____

_____

Where is the explanation of "quality points," the numbers assigned to letter grades on this campus? _____

Where do I go and to whom do I report sexual harassment or discrimination against myself? _____

_____

Where do I find information on the last day to add or drop a class? _____

_____

Bob Mahoney/The Image Works

Example: Each major has a minimum number of required courses. In addition, the major department or school may add to or alter the university's set of general education courses. If it does, you must learn this very early, preferably within the first academic term at your new university.

2. A review of the credits transferred from your current or previous college to the university.

Example: Your transfer credits will be evaluated for your admission to this university. Some may transfer directly to equivalent courses. Others will not, but you will receive "general" credit for them. Your advisor may assist you with these questions.

3. A review of the general education requirements that may still be required at the university. Sometimes more general education courses are required than you took at your previous college.

Example: Some universities have very specific courses for you to complete for your general education requirements, and there may have been no equivalent at your previous college.

4. Information on any new or additional requirements at the new institution.

Example: This may occur when the governing unit of the university determines that either new or additional courses must be completed by all incoming students. This information may not appear in your general catalog because the new requirements were adopted since the last printing.

You should check on these matters before your first academic period registration and after your enrollment or, at the latest, during the first academic term of attendance.

An advisement Electronic Bulletin Board, if provided, can be accessed directly from any computer, on campus or off, and will provide help on the most frequently asked advisement questions. Many such bulletin boards are interactive. That is, you may post a question to an advisor, and your specific question will be answered directly to you electronically (via email).

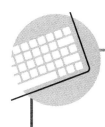

C O M P U T E R   E X E R C I S E 2.3

ADVISEMENT ELECTRONIC BULLETIN BOARD

Using the university's advisement Electronic Bulletin Board, if available, write down the icons, with brief notations, of information locations you wish to remember for quick reference in the future.

University's advisement Electronic Bulletin Board web site address:

_____

Icons or titles with brief descriptions:

_____

_____

_____

_____

_____

_____

_____

_____

_____

_____

_____

_____

CREDIT FOR WORK AT YOUR PREVIOUS SCHOOL

Transfer Credit

FAQ: I came here to get my major courses completed, and now they tell me that some of my previous courses are not going to count and I will have to take more "general education" courses! Why??

From a Community College to a Four-year University

When you transfer from a community college to a four-year university, your transcript is forwarded to evaluators. Several outcomes should be expected.

1. All the courses you took at the community college are evaluated in accordance with an "articulation" agreement between your community college and your new university.
2. Those community college courses that do not fit into the articulation agreement are, if possible, given general undergraduate level credit.
3. Alternatively, you may receive "general education certification" from your community college, which indicates completion of a major portion of your undergraduate requirements.

This certification removes the requirement for additional general education courses except those mandated by the administration or your major department. You may need to return to your community college and have it forward a certification of your general education courses to fulfill this requirement.

From One Four-year University to Another

When you transfer from one four-year university to another, your transcript follows a slightly different path.

1. Upon receipt of your application for admission to the new four-year university, the evaluators determine whether there is a general agreement on transfers between the two universities or, in some cases, between different four-year university systems.
2. Your transcript is also forwarded to the department in which you declared a major at your previous university for evaluation of your major-emphasis courses.
3. Your processing therefore involves two entities at the new university: the regular admissions office and your major department. You may expect correspondence from both when you apply. It is a very good plan to visit both offices personally, after forwarding your transcripts, so that you can clear up any possible questions.

Articulation

FAQ: What is articulation?

Articulation is a term used to describe the courses taught at another college that the four-year university will accept because it has determined their content is the same as that of specific courses that it itself offers. Articulation agreements are official contracts between a university or university system and a specific college to assist in the uniform transfer of college credits to the four-year institution.

For example, the following entry might appear in an articulation manual:

Community College A   *University AA*
  English 1 ——————————————————————————→English 101
  Math 2 ————————————————————————————→Math 102

It indicates that University AA has determined that the course English 1 at Community College A is substantially the same as English 101 on its campus and that Math 2 at the community college is the equivalent of Math 102. These "articulated" courses are for lower-division credit—generally, the 100- and 200-level courses for freshmen and sophomores. Most articulation agreements focus solely on courses to complete the student's general education requirements. The exception are those four-year institutions that have established a 2 + 2 plan with a community college.

2 + 2 Plan

FAQ: What's a 2 + 2 plan?

A 2 + 2 plan is a unique partnership between a four-year institution and a community college that permits students to begin taking lower-division (freshman and sophomore) courses in a particular major and to transfer these courses to their new university along with the general education courses also taken.

The plan is designed to provide a relatively "seamless" transfer from the community college to the four-year institution for those students who chose their majors early. However, these arrangements are normally available in only a few selected majors, such as engineering and technology. You should check with your community college counselor before transferring, and after selecting a major, to determine whether a 2 + 2 plan exists for you.

Petitioning for Transfer Credit

FAQ: They didn't give me credit for a course from my previous college that certainly looks like one in the general catalog at the university. What can I do about that?

If you believe a course you completed at the community college or other previous institution appears to be the same as one required at the university, you may, at many universities, petition for transfer credit. Your petition will be reviewed and evaluated by faculty and administrators.

However, this is a time-consuming process. Note also that

1. It will be done only at the request of the student.
2. The student must show, generally with a description of the course from the previous institution's college catalog and/or course syllabus, that the content was the same as that of a course taught at the university.
3. Generally, the petition process begins at the department in which the course is taught at the university.

Example: You believe the Geology 1 course you took at your community college is the same as Geology 101 at the university. Therefore, you put together your course description of Geology 1 from the catalog of Community College A with your course syllabus, fill out a petition, and file it with the Geology Department of the university. (This is done with the advice and consent of your academic departmental advisor.)

If the courses are indeed *very* similar, your petition will probably be granted.

General Education Certification

FAQ: A friend and I started at the same college together, but the four-year university says that we have different general education requirements. Why?

Either your previous college work was not "certified" to the four-year university (general education certification) or you had a break in your enrollment of sufficient length to require a new application.

Most colleges, in their agreements with four-year universities, will "certify" to your new university that you have successfully completed some or all of their general education requirements. This is referred to as general education certification. However, it is the responsibility of the transferring student to instruct the appropriate office at the college from which she or he is transferring to certify the transcript when it is sent forward. If this has not been done, then the evaluators at the new university must evaluate each and every course you are transferring before accepting your previous college work.

Transferred college credits considered "general education" are placed into blocks (lists) of like topics, such as American Government, which may contain one or more political science courses and history courses. The state government determines how many units must be completed before a Bachelor's Degree may be granted. Therefore, the evaluators match your previous college courses with those required by the state at your new university for compliance with general education standards adopted at the state level.

An example is the block referred to in general education as the Biological Sciences. A general education requirement at a four-year university might be to have completed three courses, two of which had to have laboratory sections. If you took those courses but were not certified for this block, then the admitting university would have to evaluate each course transferred.

Continuous Enrollment

Continuous enrollment refers to the date the student began his or her post–high school education. Most four-year universities permit students to claim, as their "contractual" requirement (general catalog) for completion of their Bachelor's Degree, their beginning quarter or semester at their previous college. If, however, there is a "break" in that enrollment (see your individual university catalog for the amount of time considered a break), the university may assign you to the "contract" of a later general catalog.

> Example: Person A and Person B enter AA Community College the same academic term of the same year. Person B drops out for a year and then returns, takes a heavy load of classes, and completes his or her AA Community College program at the same time as Person A. When both apply to University AA, however, Person A is given the general catalog (contract) of the date of her or his entry to AA Community College, whereas Person B will be given the general catalog (contract) of the year Person B *returned* to the community college. This is an example of a break in continuous enrollment that could be the answer to the Frequently Asked Question on p. 11.

REQUIREMENTS AT YOUR NEW SCHOOL

Academic Program Requirements

FAQ: Why are these general education courses required? I just want to be a firefighter!

General Education Requirements

General education courses were developed to ensure that persons graduating with a Bachelor's Degree have received information and training in a wide range of academic disciplines, from the Arts to the Sciences, that permit us to understand and appreciate our world. All universities have these requirements (1) to make graduates fully aware of the richness and diversity of their own nation and the global community of the 21st century and (2) to broaden the individual graduate's knowledge and appreciation of a wide range of academic disciplines so that he or she may understand his or her own major in a broader context and become a more well-rounded and productive member of society.

Major and Minor Requirements

Each academic major and minor, such as history or chemistry, has a specific set of courses to prepare you to be a graduate in that discipline. The term *discipline* is used to designate a specific field or study. When you meet with your departmental academic advisor you are, in effect, entering into a contract regarding your declaration to be trained in that discipline. The department will advise you of the course and grade point requirements you must fulfill to earn that degree. A similar set of "contractual" obligations exists for someone choosing that academic discipline as a minor. A major indicates what your *primary* course of study was and that you completed your training in this area. A minor acknowledges *basic* training in the academic discipline, but it is not a statement by the department that you completed training in the area.

 FAQ: This new grade report is confusing!

Interpreting the Grade Report

Each four-year institution issues a grade report at the completion of the academic period. Some new terms may be included:

Earned hours are the total units completed to date, including those not used toward a degree program.

Quality hours are the total units completed in the student's degree program.

Quality points are the numeric sum of points earned for all courses taken. This is computed by multiplying the number of units the student earns for a course (example, a 4-unit course) by the assigned value of the grade received (such as 3.7, the quality points for an A– on a 4.0-point Plus-Minus grading scale). See the GPA examples below.

Grade Point Calculation

Using the calculation system described above, it is possible to caculate the GPA for a student's current academic period and a cumulative academic GPA. Universities generally report this information to the student.

If your university does not issue such a report, you can compute it as follows:

1. Using the "quality points" formula, compute the quality points for each course taken.
2. Sum these quality points for all courses taken during the academic period.
3. Divide this total by the total number of units completed.

Example: Student ZZ Top has the following grade report. He attends a four-year institution with a 4.0-point Plus-Minus grading system where

A = 4	B+ = 3.3	C+ = 2.3
A− = 3.7	B = 3.0	C = 2.0
	B− = 2.7	C− = 1.7

ZZ Top's GRADE REPORT

Course	Units	Grade	Quality Points	
Sociology 102	4	A−	(3.7×4)	= 14.8
Biology 155	4	B	(3.0×4)	= 12.0
Physics 101	4	C	(2.0×4)	= 8.0
Physical Ed 101	1	A	(4.0×1)	= 4.0
Total units	13		Total	= 38.8 quality points

ZZ Top's GPA for this academic period is 38.8 quality points divided by 13 units, or 2.98.

Deficiency Points

Students must keep a current account of their grade point averages, because falling below the acceptable level of C, or 2.0, on the 4.0-point grading system generates "deficiency points." This means that a student whose cumulative quality points are not sufficient to generate the minimum is at risk of one or more administrative or academic sanctions.

Example: A student who completes 12 units in an academic term but earns only 20 quality points has deficiency points. Because the minimum GPA is 2.0 for all courses taken, this student has 4 deficiency points.

(Computation: 12 units times 2.0, the quality value for a minimum C average, yields 24 quality points.)

This deficiency puts the student into a special relationship with the university, because the original "contract" was for the student to maintain the minimum GPA. If this happens to you,

1. Your financial aid will be impacted, because you are not maintaining the minimum GPA required to sustain it.
2. Your "continuous enrollment" designation will be in jeopardy, which means that unless you take care of this immediately or within one academic term, you may have to begin your contract with the university under a new set of rules—a new general catalog of requirements.

Academic Probation

FAQ: My grade report indicates that I am on academic probation. Why and how do I get off probation?

Four-year institutions have two classifications for students who become deficient either academically or administratively. Those who are academically deficient may be placed on academic probation, or if they have not complied with a series of academic requirements, may be academically disqualified.

Each university system has a set of guidelines to determine successful progress toward a degree. *Probation* is a term used to advise the student that a grade point deficiency exists—that is, the minimum GPA to remain a continuing student, which is usually a C (2.0), has not been maintained. Therefore, the student is placed on **academic probation** and is given a specified number of academic periods to correct this (check the general catalog for specifics). It is the student's responsibility to initiate the corrective action required. If you are in this position, you should seek assistance from your academic advisor.

Academic Disqualification

A student who receives notification of **academic disqualification** on a grade report and in a letter from the school will not be permitted to register for classes at that time. Conditions for re-admittance or reinstatement will be found in the general catalog and must be met if the student is to remain a continuing student. However, reinstatement is not automatic and this notification may result in the student's not being readmitted to the university.

FAQ: How can I correct this?

Reinstatement

In most institutions, disqualified students may submit, to the appropriate school dean or department chair, a petition for immediate reinstatement. If the reinstatement is granted, such students are frequently placed on some type of special probation, particularly if they have more deficiency points than are allowed for a continuing student.

Academic Holds

Sometimes when students attempt to register, usually through an automated telephone system or via the Internet, they find that their request is denied because an **academic hold** has been placed on them.

This means that until they clear up whatever deficiency exists in their academic requirements, they will not be permitted to register. Usually this indicates some incomplete or missing administrative data. If the hold is for an academic reason, such as overall grade point average, the student must initiate corrective action immediately. (See your general catalog.)

Other possible reasons include an unpaid fine for an overdue book at the library, an unpaid laboratory fee, and failure to have a current tuberculosis X-ray on file at the student health center. As soon as the student satisfies these requirements, he or she will be permitted to continue to register. The student should promptly contact the office that initiated the hold and/or her or his major advisor. Students on academic hold should contact their academic advisor to evaluate the options.

Academic Renewal

FAQ: How can I correct an academic hold?

Many academic institutions have a program that will permit a student to repeat a course—that is, to take it over—if the original course grade was less than the minimum acceptable to remain in good standing (usually a C). These repetitions must be taken at the same institution. However, there is always a limit on the number of repetitions which will be allowed. Again, check your general catalog for specifics.

The student must initiate this action by filing whatever form is required by the university. Note that your second grade for this course will be the one computed into your grade point average, although the first will also remain on your transcript.

The Enrollment Process

Enrollment indicates that you have been accepted as a member of the learning community of this university. The following sections detail the various processes you may undergo.

Enrollment Categories

Your category of enrollment reflects the record of your academic preparation for this particular institution. A "regularly admitted student" is fully qualified academically, for example, whereas "special admission" means that the entering student must complete some academic requirements in a specified time to be permitted continued enrollment at this university. Your enrollment category is made clear in your letter of admission.

Registration

Registration is the process of being officially admitted to the roster of specific courses at the university for this academic period.

Early registration is an opportunity to register for your courses before the rest of the general student body. This is an option granted to students with special needs and sometimes to athletes, student government officers, and others. Check with your academic advisor or the general catalog.

Late Enrollment or Registration

Late enrollment or registration will be treated as a special condition. You must check your general catalog or departmental advisor for the specifics at your university.

COMPUTER EXERCISE 2.4

DEPARTMENTAL WEB PAGE

Using your major department's web page, if available, write down the icons, with brief notations, for locations you may wish to consult for information in the future.

Department's web site address:

_____

Icons or titles with brief descriptions:

_____

_____

_____

_____

_____

_____

_____

_____

_____

_____

_____

_____

_____

EXERCISE 2.5

SCAVENGER HUNT

It is important for you to acquaint yourself with the campus community and the various services that different offices provide. This exercise is a scavenger hunt. You are to find the location and services provided for students at each of the following places. Record, with brief notations, the location of each resource and the basic service it provides.

Your Student Health Center. Where is it? What level of service can you receive (e.g., pharmacy, counseling, immunizations)? _____

_____

_____

Your Student-access Computer Centers on Campus. Where are they? What are their hours of operation? What word processing and spreadsheet programs are available? Can you send email from there? _____

_____

_____

Your University Library. What types of services are available for students? Free inter-library loans for books and journal articles? Library instruction courses? Style manuals for writing? _____

_____

_____

Your Student Tutorial Center. Where is it? What subjects are available? How do you register? Who can register? How many times may you see a tutor? _____

_____

_____

Your Student Writing Center. Where is it? What services are available? How do you register? Who can register? How many times may you use it during an academic period?

_____

_____

Your Financial Aid Office. Where is it? What are its hours of operation? What types of financial assistance does it provide? How do you sign up or enroll? _____

_____

_____

Your Center for Student Life. What extracurricular activities does it coordinate for students? What does it provide? Discounted tickets? Trips? On-campus entertainment? Where is it? _____

_____

_____

Your Ethnic Student Resource Centers. What do they provide for you? Who may join and participate? When are they open? Where are they?_____

_____

_____

Your Campus Religious Centers or Meditation Facilities. Where are they? When are they open? What groups are available? Who may participate? When are their meetings or services? _____

_____

_____

Your Student Government. Where is it located? What does it do? How can you participate? Who may run for office? How do you register to run or vote? _____

_____

_____

Your Student Newspaper. Where is it located? How do you get articles about your group entered as feature stories? _____

_____

_____

Your Office for Students with Disabilities (Challenges). Where do students with special challenges, such as physical or learning disabilities, go for assistance? What types of services do they receive?_____

_____

_____

CHAPTER 3

Campus Relationships

You've often heard the phrase "When in Rome, do as the Romans do." Indeed, it is important for you, as a transfer student, to ascertain the norms of your new environment and conform as best you can to those expectations. Your institution has a set of norms, or expected behaviors. Usually, those who successfully abide by their social group's norms achieve success, and those who defy these rules are penalized.

RULES OF CONDUCT: HOW TO SUCCEED IN YOUR NEW ENVIRONMENT

Are these rules of expected behavior published in a booklet? Usually not. They are the unwritten rules of conduct governing relationships in your new environment. The purpose of this chapter is to give you a "heads up" on some of these unspoken rules to minimize the number of toes you might step on by simply not understanding how you are expected to act.

 FAQ: What are the norms for college behavior?

Although there will be some variation from campus to campus and from region to region, there are some basic rules that you should follow.

The Ten Commandments of College Behavior

1. **Thou shalt attend class.**
    Class attendance is important. Some instructors take roll; others don't. Instructors usually state in their syllabus whether your attendance will be considered in determining your final course grade. But beware: Even if a portion of your grade is not formally based on your attendance record, it still counts. If you miss a class, chances are you will miss important course material. Many instructors lecture on material not contained in your

books. You could also miss an important announcement or assignment. Borrowing someone's notes is not the same as being present in class.

FAQ: What if I have to miss class for an important, legitimate reason?

If you know in advance that you will have to miss a class, inform your instructor ahead of time and ask whether there will be any special announcements or assignments. This conveys that there is a legitimate reason why you must miss a particular class. Just as important, it reflects a mature, courteous attitude and determination not to get behind in your course work.

2. Thou shalt not put any other events before thy college requirements and commitments.

Do not miss an exam or due date. You can't imagine how many excuses professors get on exam days and on days when assignments and papers are due. The old "My dog ate my homework" has been replaced by more creative and emotional tales of woe. How about "My roommate's boyfriend broke up with her, and I had to calm her down to prevent her from hurting herself"? Or "I had just finished my paper when my computer crashed and I lost the whole thing"?

We all know that sometimes, and we emphasize the word *sometimes,* things happen. Unexpected, catastrophic events that are beyond one's control do occur. You could be felled by an unexpected illness (such as appendicitis), or there could be a death in your immediate family. If a crisis occurs, get hold of your instructor ASAP. Use voicemail or email. Leave a contact number. Explain the problem, and state that you will bring verification of it.

FAQ: What if I'm not sure my instructor will accept my excuse?

If you are not sure whether your instructor will treat your excuse as a valid reason to miss an exam or assignment, you should contact that instructor immediately and explain the situation. Most professors are reasonable and will try their best to deal fairly with the situation. The important points here are to inform your instructor immediately, to be truthful about the circumstances involved, and to provide verification.

3. Thou shalt make friends in class.

Use the buddy system. For every class you have, make sure you befriend at least one person. Exchange names, email addresses, and phone numbers. Then, if you ever can't make it to class, you will have someone to call to find out what you've missed. Be sure to select a classmate who is responsible and reliable and who will attend class on a regular basis. This means you owe the same obligation and responsibility to your classmate.

4. Thou shalt take personal responsibility for thy life.

If you miss a class for whatever reason, it is your responsibility to find out what you've missed. It is not the instructor's responsibility to contact you to communicate important material. If an assignment was given out on the day you were not in class, the excuse that you weren't there that day is *not* a valid excuse for not doing the work. It's up to you to find out what you have missed. If the buddy system fails, visit or call your professor. If your professor is not in, leave a message that you came by or called and that you will try again to reach him or her.

5. Thou shall be on time for the start of class.

Don't be tardy. Some instructors penalize you for being tardy. Others lock the classroom door at the beginning of the class session. Of course, in large lecture halls your absence or tardiness is less likely to be noticed by the instructor—unless you fall over three people getting to your seat. On the other hand, being late or absent in small classes is obvious. If you exhibit chronic tardiness, you are communicating to your instructor that you don't take the course seriously. Remember, it's your instructor who determines your final grade, so you don't want to engage in any behavior that leaves the impression that you don't care about a topic that he or she has spent a lifetime studying.

 FAQ: My classes are spread out across campus and I can't get to class on time. What should I do?

When scheduling your classes, keep in mind the time allocated between classes and the distance you will have to travel from class to class. Be realistic about your ability to traverse the campus in this short period of time. If it is unavoidable and you are not able to get to class on time, inform your instructor of your problem. Being one or two minutes late might be workable; anything more than that really depends on the good graces of your instructor.

6. Thou shalt be aware of the sun's movement across the sky.

Wear a watch. If you're not used to wearing a watch and being on time, this is a good time to start. If you are chronically late, set your watch 15 minutes ahead of time. Even though you know what you've done, it still works. Go figure! You don't want to be late for class or late for meetings where your classmates are depending on you.

7. Thou shalt not speak idly.

Don't talk in class. Some instructors are more forgiving and tolerant of chatterers than others. When an instructor is lecturing, she or he wants to look out at the room and see students who are riveted and engrossed—or at least daydreaming silently. Even if you're not interested, learn to pretend. Why go out of your way to antagonize a person who will award your grade in the class? On a simpler level, lengthy lapses of attention are just plain rude. If you have a question or need clarification on the material, ask the instructor, not your neighbor. Never, *ever* fall asleep in class, and don't let out huge loud yawns.

8. Honor thy professor and teaching assistants.

Address your professors with respect. Never call your instructor by his or her first name unless you have been given permission to do so. Always use their professional title of Professor or Dr.

FAQ: I'm not sure whether my instructor has a Ph.D. Should I still address him as Dr.?

Many instructors do not have Ph.D.'s. For your instructors who don't have doctorates, you cannot go wrong by addressing them as Professor. When in doubt, "Professor" is the appropriate title.

9. Thou shalt take the time to know the correct sequence of letters in thy professor's name.

Don't misspell your instructor's name. Your instructor's name is on the course syllabus, and misspelling it indicates sloppiness and inattention.

10. Thou shalt remember that thou obtainist more bees with honey than with vinegar.

Always be polite. On campus you will have to interact with administrators, faculty, and staff. At times your interaction with campus personnel can be potentially volatile. It is in your interest always to act considerately. Be persistent, but don't threaten or intimidate, no matter how frustrating the situation. Be polite and courteous at all times. Most people are more likley to respond cooperatively to polite behavior than to "boorish" behavior.

VISITING WITH FACULTY

Office Hours

All faculty are required to hold office hours, during which they remain in their offices for meetings with students. On most campuses, faculty have regularly scheduled office hours. These hours are usually stated on the course syllabus and are often posted on the professor's office door. Some instructors prefer that you make an appointment to see them during office hours; others have a drop-in policy. Determine which system is appropriate for which instructor.

Make it a habit to visit each of your professors at least once a term. Drop by more often if need be. If you have an appointment that you are unable to keep, notify your professor ahead of time and reschedule.

FAQ: I really like my professor and would like to talk to her about things in general and to let her know how much I'm enjoying her class. Is it okay for me to visit during office hours for this purpose?

E X E R C I S E   3.1

THE BUDDY SYSTEM

For each of your courses, select at least one classmate who will be your contact person in the event that you have to miss a class. Exchange names, email addresses, and telephone numbers.

Course _____

Contact person(s)_____

Email address _____

Telephone number _____

Course _____

Contact person(s)_____

Email address _____

Telephone number _____

Course _____

Contact person(s)_____

Email address _____

Telephone number _____

Course _____

Contact person(s)_____

Email address _____

Telephone number _____

Absolutely! Professors love to hear how well they are doing and that students are engaged and enjoying the course. Many faculty welcome students who want to stop by just to chat (look out, we are implying that professors are people too). If in doubt whether your instructor is receptive to this type of visit, ask casually whether it would be okay to make an appointment just to talk.

The Office Visit

Okay, so now you're going to visit your professor. What are the expectations? First, if you made an appointment, be on time. If you are late, your instructor may not be able to see you because of other appointments or commitments. Second, come prepared. If you want to discuss your performance on your last

Brian Smith/Stock Boston

exam, be sure to bring your exam with you. Likewise, if you want some guidance on your term paper, bring your work along. For advice on your schedule and on what courses to take, bring the schedule of classes and school catalog with you. For graduation checks or other issues requiring forms and paperwork, make sure you arrive with all necessary forms and documentation. Don't waste your and your professor's time by not being prepared. Not only will your professor appreciate your thoroughness, but you will get what you came for—an answer to your question or a solution to your problem.

FAQ: I have a professor who makes me very nervous. I have to visit him during office hours to get help with my paper. How should I handle this situation?

By all means, keep your appointment. There are steps you can take to alleviate the stress associated with this visit. First, come prepared. Have a written list of questions you want to discuss with your instructor. Consult your list once you are in the office. If you are uncomfortable being alone with your instructor, keep the office door open. If it is closed, ask politely whether you may open it. Then do so. You don't need to convey any concern, fear, or distrust. Just suggest that you are warm, or the office feels stuffy, or any other similar reason you can come up with. At the conclusion of your visit, thank your instructor for his or her time.

FAQ: My instructor doesn't show up for office hours. This has happened on a number of occasions. What should I do?

Unfortunately, some faculty do not keep to their designated office hours. This is unfair to students who arrange their schedules to meet with their professors. Contact your instructor after the missed meeting and ask to reschedule. If another meeting is missed without any prior explanation or arrangements having been made, contact the department chair to discuss the situation. If the department chair is unavailable, contact the dean of the school or college.

Visits via Email

Just as more students are using their computers to become productive, more and more professors are using their computers to communicate with their students via email. Usually, your instructor will announce to the class whether this is preferable or practical. If your instructor welcomes email communication, make sure you have his or her correct email address.

Communicate via email with the same formality and politeness that you would exhibit in face-to-face interactions. Address your instructor as Professor or Dr. Don't get too personal. For some students, this channel of communication is preferable to actual office visits. They are less nervous and can speak more freely. For others, there is no substitute for meeting in person. Choose the method of communication that works best for you.

 FAQ: Is it okay to call or email my professor at home?

Only if your instructor has given you permission. Otherwise, respect your professors' privacy and do not contact them at home.

OFF-CAMPUS RELATIONSHIPS WITH FACULTY, STAFF, OR ADMINISTRATORS

Every campus has strict guidelines governing contacts between students and faculty, staff, or administrators both on and off campus. Your general catalog will identify these for your campus, but in general, "social" meetings are discouraged unless they represent an approved departmental group gathering.

 FAQ: What if I think I would like to date one of my instructors?

EXERCISE 3.2

FACULTY CONTACT NUMBERS

It is important to have a list of all your instructors and the ways you can contact them in case of an emergency. It is also advisable to have not only each professor's telephone number and email address but also a department office number to use if you need to leave an urgent message. Write down each instructor's office telephone number, email address, department office number, and office hours. Keep a copy of this list with you at all times.

Professor _____

Office telephone number_____

Email address _____

Department office telephone number _____

Office hours _____

Professor _____

Office telephone number _____

Email address _____

Department office telephone number _____

Office hours _____

Professor _____

Office telephone number_____

Email address _____

Department office telephone number _____

Office hours _____

Professor _____

Office telephone number_____

Email address _____

Department office telephone number _____

Office hours _____

EXERCISE 3.3

INTERVIEW AN INSTRUCTOR

Visit one of your instructors. Select one with a Ph.D. (you want to get used to interact-ing in a one-on-one situation with a "Dr."). After your visit, fill in the following ac-count of the experience.

a. Professor's name _____

b. Date and time visited _____

c. What was discussed? _____

_____

_____

_____

_____

d. How would you describe your experience? What was the best part of your visit? What was the worst part, if any? _____

_____

_____

_____

_____

Individual "social" meetings, although they do occur, are not encouraged. This is for the protection of the faculty, administrators, and staff, as well as of the student. The reason is to avoid a situation in which an unscrupulous uni-versity person might try to take advantage of the student, or the student might try to "blackmail" the university person even if nothing immoral or illegal transpired.

The question of romance between a university person, such as a member of the faculty, administration, or staff, and a student may arise. On some campuses, campus codes of behavior forbid romantic relationships between faculty and stu-dents. On other campuses, these relationships are regulated. If any university em-ployee, faculty member, administrator, or staff person romantically involved with a student is that student's instructor, advisor, or mentor or will have any im-pact on the student's academic career through grading, letters of reference, or

COMPUTER EXERCISE 3.4

WEB SITES ON ROMANTIC OR SEXUAL RELATIONSHIPS WITH FACULTY OR OTHER ADMINISTRATIVE STAFF ON CAMPUS

These World Wide Web sites will acquaint you with this perennial problem. By referring to these sites, you will understand that *you are not alone, nor need you be a victim.* After reading the information at the sites, and if you are a victim or feel intimidated, contact your campus women's resource center, or, if you are male, your campus student center, for referral and assistance.

All of these sites were located on the search engine **www.altavista.com** by using the search terms found below in the "search box." Not all references will be directly related to your situation, so record any notes you find relevant, and then *report* whatever is causing you concern.

Sexual relationships on campus

_____

_____

Romantic relationships on campus

_____

_____

Student relationships on campus

_____

_____

recommendation for awards, then that faculty member *must* remove himself or herself from participation in any decision regarding that student.

WORKING WITH UNIVERSITY STAFF

Students will come in contact with staff members in many situations during their academic career. A simple rule is to treat everyone with whom you interact with respect—the same respect you expect for yourself.

There are different levels of staff, just as there are different levels of faculty. In any office, the staff will usually be hierarchically organized: receptionist, clerk, administrative assistant, and/or departmental secretary. You should respectfully begin your inquiries with the first level of staff made available to you.

Processing Upon Your Arrival on Campus

In most instances, you will be processed by professional staff without an advanced academic degree. These persons will ensure that all of your paperwork has been processed—from transfer of credits to financial aid. Again, be courteous and be prepared. Always go to these meetings or offices with all the paperwork you may be required to produce.

Processing During Your Academic Term(s) on Campus

In these instances, you may be required to meet with either an administrator or an academician with a Master's Degree or a doctorate. Go to the meeting prepared, but remember that the academician's staff, secretary, or assistant can help in your preparation for the meeting and your processing afterward. Again, respect for the other is the watchword.

PREJUDICE AND DISCRIMINATION

Our campuses mirror our society. Therefore, you will encounter people whose early life experiences or social learning have fostered prejudicial attitudes and even discriminatory behavior toward those unlike themselves.

In the past, such attitudes and behaviors were actual barriers to some students' successful completion of an academic program. However, civil rights laws prohibit such behavior now.

 FAQ: What do I do if I think I am being harassed or discriminated against?

All campuses have reporting mechanisms for these violations. The university will investigate, and the perpetrator will be dealt with either at the university level or by the civil authorities (police and courts). Check your student handbook or student guide for the procedure to follow in reporting the incident. *Do not* ignore it and assume it will go away if you don't take action. Report *any* harassment or discriminatory treatment on the part of *anyone* at the university: student, instructor, staff, or administrator. Refer to Exercise 3.6 for address and telephone numbers of the offices where your complaint should be lodged.

Universities are committed to the principle of equality of opportunity for all individuals. This commitment requires that no discrimination shall occur in any program or activity of the university on the basis of race, color, religion, national origin, sex, sexual orientation (in some states), marital status, pregnancy, age, disability, disabled veteran status, Viet Nam–era veteran status, or any other classification that may preclude a person's being considered as an individual and judged on individual merit.

Campus Speech/Behavior Codes

Some campuses have developed speech and behavior codes to govern what is acceptable among members of the university community. Although some of these codes have been challenged in federal court, many are still operational. They are designed to prohibit the use of negative words, phrases, or forms of address to demean or belittle another person or group. A student judicial board generally administers such codes, with review by the university.

All students should check their general catalog for information regarding this or other nondiscrimination programs at their campus.

Cults

In the United States, we celebrate our right to religious freedom and the expression thereof. However, there are some groups that form under the banner of religion but constitute what in psychoanalytic descriptions are referred to as cults. These organizations frequent college campuses because they seek recruits among the young and eager to learn but lonely students.

Your campus counseling center or student health center can give you information on the techniques used by such groups and, in some cases, the traumatic effects on the individual. Some susceptible students drop out of school, associate only with members of the cult, suspend contact with family and friends, and may even live communally with their new group and give it all their income. Although this is their constitutional right, giving themselves over to the group can result in emotional problems for the cult member. Your campus counseling and student health service staff are equipped to assist you if you are experiencing anxiety, depression, or guilt and are unable to function because of these feelings.

E X E R C I S E   3.5

CONFLICT RESOLUTION

This is an in-class exercise. In small groups, engage in the following role-playing exercises. Then, for each role-playing scenario, have one group member write down a description of the problem and how the group solved it in the role-playing exercise. After each group performs, the members should report to the class on the specific problems and solutions arrived at by their group.

a. Role-play the expressing of a prejudicial attitude and the correct response

b. Role-play a discriminatory behavior and the correct response

E X E R C I S E   3.6

UNIVERSITY CONTACTS FOR DISCRIMINATION

List the offices or individuals on your campus that you should contact if you experience any form of discrimination.

Campus office _____

Contact person _____

Telephone number _____

C O M P U T E R   E X E R C I S E   3.7

WORLD WIDE WEB SITES ON DISCRIMINATION

The following World Wide Web sites offer some additional information on the insidious practice of discrimination. Not every listing deals directly with students. Some sites are listed because they include references to web sites or books that do.

Using the following descriptors in the "search" box on **www.altavista.com,** enter the web site address given for each.

Racial discrimination on campus _____

Homosexual discrimination on campus _____

Sexism discrimination on campus _____

Religious bigotry discrimination on campus _____

Classism discrimination on campus _____

Physical disability discrimination on campus _____

Of course, these sources show you only what has been done or is being done on other campuses. You must consult your own Student Affairs Office, Office for Students with Disabilities, Equal Opportunity Office, Sexual Harassment Office, or other center that deals with these issues on your campus. The purpose of becoming familiar with these sites is to realize that no one who becomes a target of discrimination is alone. *Something can be done!*

STRATEGIES FOR ACADEMIC SUCCESS

CHAPTER 4

Time Management

THE CULTURAL SENSE OF TIME

Everyone has a sense of time that is not based on a clock or timepiece. In our society, being on time and the resulting sense of urgency mark every activity. Consequently, many people say that they have no time for themselves or that they had no time to study or that there are too many other demands on their time. But time is a knowable, predictable resource. You're in control! Let's consider why time is such a significant part of a student's life.

Moving from a Semester System to a Quarter System, or Vice Versa

Let's look at two hypothetical scenarios for your transfer to a different academic time system.

First, imagine that you are back at your previous college and that it operated on a semester system: approximately 15 weeks of instruction and the final-examination week. Remember that history class that just seemed to go on and on and on? Now, imagine you are at your new university, which is on a quarter system: approximately 10 weeks of instruction and the final-examination week. You will cover the same amount of material as at your semester-system school but in much less time. By the end of the first week of the quarter, the instructor has assigned your first assignment. By the end of the fourth week (the fifth at the latest), you will have taken your midterm exam!

Moving from a semester system to a quarter system can be a shock. Assuming that you meet twice a week at your quarter-system school, by the *second* class period you are taking serious notes. This is decidedly different from the semester approach to which you were accustomed.

Now imagine that you were at a quarter-system school and are moving to a school that operates on a semester system. All your friends have told you that because of the "extra" weeks, you will have lots more time to relax before getting serious about studying.

EXERCISE 4.1

TIME MANAGEMENT SCALE

0	1 2 3	4 5 6	7 8 9	10
Never	Sometimes	Frequently	Most of the time	Always

_____ 1. I am indispensable. I find myself taking on various tasks because I'm the only one who can do them.

_____ 2. Daily crises take up all my time. I have no time to do important things because I am too busy putting out fires.

_____ 3. I attempt to do too much at one time. I feel I can do it all, and I rarely say "no."

_____ 4. I feel unrelenting pressure, as though I'm always behind and have no way to catch up. I'm always rushing.

_____ 5. I habitually work long hours: 10, 12, 14, or more hours a day, 5, 6, or even 7 days a week.

_____ 6. I am constantly overwhelmed by demands and details and feel that I have to do what I don't want to do most of the time.

_____ 7. I feel guilty about leaving work or school on time. I don't have sufficient time for rest or personal relationships. I take worries and problems home.

_____ 8. I constantly miss deadlines.

_____ 9. I am plagued by fatigue and listlessness with many slack hours of unproductive activity.

_____ 10. I chronically vacillate between unpleasant alternatives.

_____ TOTAL SCORE

The higher your score, the more important you see time in shaping your life, even at the expense of doing a good job at the task undertaken.

This is probably the most difficult situation. Although you have more time in terms of weeks, your responsibilities and the quality of work expected do not diminish. Rather, given the "extra" time, your instructors have a right to expect even more rigorous work. That is, they will expect even more detail—and perhaps more assignments—because of their ability to expand on the details of the subject. This is _not_ the time to relax. On the contrary, it is the time to focus more sharply on your subjects because your instructors will be elaborating more.

Mark Richards/PhotoEdit

Assessing Your Use of Time

You have been taught that time is a very important element of your life and that you need to account for every minute of it. This is so much a part of our culture that we often run from event to event or activity to activity in the service of time, not for the activity itself. We very often find it more important to be able to provide a list of the many activities we have undertaken than to take satisfaction in our accomplishments or even our understanding of what we did.

Before we can help you overcome your "time shock" upon moving between academic periods, we need to have you examine your ideas about time. Exercise 4.1 asks you to assess your attitude toward time.

Our Real Allocation of Time

Let us peer into the life of a hypothetical student named Abelard and see how he actually utilizes his time. In Exercise 4.2, you will complete the same sort of summary of your use of time.

Abelard has the following priorities, although not necessarily in this order: obtain a college degree, work to support himself, an interpersonal relationship, and time for "his things," including friends. These priorities are typical of many of today's college students. In the following account of Abelard's week, times are shown on a 24-hour clock, where 1300 is one p.m., 2400 is midnight, etc.

ABELARD'S DAY

	Monday	Tuesday
0600–0700	sleep	sleep
0700–0800	arise and get ready	arise and get ready
0800–0900	travel to school	travel to school
0900–1000	see friends	study at library
1000–1100	class	study at library
1100–1200	class	lunch with friends
1200–1300 (noon–1 p.m.)	lunch	video games
1300–1400	pool room	class
1400–1500	class	class
1500–1600	class	drive to work
1600–1700	drive to work	work at McDonald's
1700–1800	work at McDonald's	work at McDonald's
1800–1900	work at McDonald's	work at McDonald's
1900–2000	drive home	drive home
2000–2100	watch TV, answer email and voice mail, study	watch TV, answer email and voice mail, study
2100–2200	watch TV, answer email and voice mail, study	watch TV, answer email and voice mail, study
2200–2300	talk to girlfriend	talk to girlfriend
2300–2400	talk to girlfriend sleep	talk to girlfriend sleep

Now we need to examine how Abelard utilized his available time and for which priorities. How did he do?

Priority One: Getting a College Degree

Attend class	1000–1200 and 1400–1600 on Monday	
Study at library	0900–1100 on Tuesday	
Attend class	1300–1500 on Tuesday	
Total class and study time		8 hours
Travel time to school	0800–0900 for two days	2 hours

We cannot add the time from 2000 (8 p.m.) to 2200 (10 p.m.) as study time, because one *cannot* study while occupying one's mind and body with other activities.

Total time spent toward getting a college degree = 10 hours

Priority Two: Working to Support Yourself

Monday 1600 (4 p.m.) to 2000 (8 p.m.) including drive time

Tuesday 1500 (3 p.m.) to 2000 (8 p.m.) including drive time

Total time spent on working to support himself = 9 hours

Priority Three: "His Things"

See friends	0900–1000 on Monday
Pool room	1300–1400 on Monday
Lunch with friends and video games	1100–1300 on Tuesday
Watch TV, answer email and voice mail	2000–2200 Monday and Tuesday

Total time spent on "his things" = 8 hours

Priority Four: Interpersonal Relationship

Talk to girlfriend	2200–2400 Monday and Tuesday

Total time spent on interpersonal relationship = 4 hours

Thus a three-item priority list emerges from Abelard's allocation of time.

First	Getting a college degree
Two priorities rank second	Working to support himself and enjoying "his things"
Third	Interpersonal relationship

Please complete Exercise 4.2 to help you understand *your* allocation of the time in your day. By honestly completing this exercise, you can help yourself assess your real priorities for your life and your current academic situation.

Remember to include all of your activities for a two-day period: Monday and Tuesday of any week of your school year. Also note that at the conclusion, you are to summarize by category how you spent that time. You will then know what your priorities for time are by the amount of time you allot to each of the activities.

Most people spend more time on "their things" than on other activities. As a student you must reorder the priorities and tell others, including your significant other or employer, that you need flexible hours to be with them and uninterrupted time for your academic work.

E X E R C I S E 4.2

DAILY CALENDAR OF ACTIVITIES

Summarize all of your activities during these time periods for Monday and Tuesday of the same week. Use extra pages if necessary.

	Monday	Tuesday
0700–0800		
0800–0900		
0900–1000		
1000–1100		
1100–1200		
1200–1300		
1300–1400		
1400–1500		
1500–1600		
1600–1700		
1700–1800		
1800–1900		
1900–2000		
2000–2100		
2100–2200		
2200–2300		
2300–2400		

Scoring and Interpretation. Now categorize your activities in terms of your apparent priorities. How much time did you use for each of the following activities? (Summarize by major activity and number of hours to the closest half-hour for each activity.)

Getting a college degree (including studying—2 hours for each classroom hour—and transportation to and from school)

_____

Working to support yourself (including transportation to and from work)

_____

"Your things" (television, hanging out, etc.)

_____

Interpersonal relationships (significant others)

_____

Interpretation: What does your allocation of time say about your priorities? Do your hourly allocations surprise you?

Now review your allocation of time. How can you (or should you) reallocate time to fit the priorities you think you have? Then write down the reason why you must reorder your allocation of time, and place this note near your telephone, beside your computer monitor, or in another location where you spend time that could be allocated more productively to "getting your college degree."

Restructuring Your Study Area

Let us examine where you study—the physical setting of your study time, which we refer to as a study area.

Let's find a place to study successfully. Where can this area be located? Students may find study areas set aside in cubicles in their university library and, in some cases, in specialized areas of their student union or commons. Some schools will permit you to utilize unoccupied classrooms. The key is to have privacy: *no friends* except those actively engaged in studying as well.

Other students prefer to study at home or in their dorm room or apartment. The desk or table in such residences is frequently a multipurpose piece of furniture. When studying, you must *convert* this furniture to study use. Do this by (1) physically moving it to another location and/or rotating it 180 to 270 degrees, (2) removing everything that is not study material from the desk or table and out of sight of the person studying, and (3) moving appropriate lighting to the study area, if necessary.

At the conclusion of this study time, the furniture must be returned to its former utilitarian location, and the items pertinent to that function must be replaced. *At no time* should the furniture involved in some utilitarian task and the study task be intermixed. Adhering to this rule reinforces in your mind—and in those of others—that this configuration is for study and no other activity.

Quality of Study Time: Privacy

We will now examine the actual time-to-study minutes utilized in this study area. You must not permit others to interrupt your study time. This time should be announced in advance to your employer, your family, your significant other, and your friends.

They must also understand that during this time you will not answer telephone calls (standard or cellular), nor will you respond to pages or accept unannounced visitors. No familial tasks or chores, such as baby-sitting, should be expected either. Emphasize to all that if they respect you as a person seeking a higher education, they must honor your student time as well.

Preparation

Because you have specified a "study only" area with appropriate furniture and lighting and have designated a private time, you must be ready by having *all* the materials you are going to need on hand at your study site. This will include your textbook(s), notes, and copies of readings from the reserve desk, if appropriate. Your Internet connection, if you have a computer at home, should be up and online.

Now you are ready to *use* this time set aside for study. Allocation of time should be in blocks of 1 hour or greater for original study and in blocks of not less than 30 minutes for a review of work previously read or taken as notes.

A block of time is an uninterrupted period of time: *no* interruptions for other tasks; for answering telephone calls, cell phones, or pagers; or for personal interactions (conversations) with others. Complete Exercise 4.6 to test your mastery of this.

E X E R C I S E   4.3

PLAN A TIME SCHEDULE

Situation A

You are a transfer student at this school. You have the following academic schedule and work commitments. Create a time management plan for yourself.

Courses:

Sociology 201-01	Principles of Sociology	MW 0950–1130
Sociology 120-05	Intimate Relations	Th 0800–0940
English 096-04	Basic Writing II	MW 0800–0940

You work at McDonald's Monday through Friday from 1:00 p.m. to 6:00 p.m. You must take care of your two siblings, ages 11 and 12, on Saturday mornings—that is, until noon.

   Prepare a time management schedule. Don't forget to allow yourself some personal time!

Situation B

You are a transfer student at this school. You have the following academic schedule and work commitments. Work out a time management plan for yourself.

Courses:

Speech 150-02	Oral Communication	MW 0800–0940
Biology 155-01	Animal Biology	MW 1215–1330
Biology 155-02	Biology Laboratory	M 1340–1630
English 095-21	Basic Writing I	Th 0800–0940

You work at Shakey's Pizza Friday through Sunday from 8 a.m. to 6 p.m. (with an hour break).

   Let us examine your holistic understanding of these exercises on time management. At this point, complete Exercise 4.3, in which you will set up a schedule, applying what we have learned thus far about time management.

   Now, let's interpret the time schedules you prepared for these two situations. (If you worked in groups, give your group's solutions to another group for comment.) Consider the following in your evaluation:

1. Was enough time—and time in the appropriate blocks (number of minutes)—allocated for study? Assume 1 to 2 hours of study for each hour of class time.

EXERCISE 4.3 Continued

DAILY CALENDAR FOR SITUATION A

Summarize all activities during these time periods for Monday and Tuesday of the same week.

	Monday	Tuesday
0700–0800		
0800–0900		
0900–1000		
1000–1100		
1100–1200		
1200–1300		
1300–1400		
1400–1500		
1500–1600		
1600–1700		
1700–1800		
1800–1900		
1900–2000		
2000–2100		
2100–2200		
2200–2300		
2300–2400		

DAILY CALENDAR FOR SITUATION B

Summarize all activities during these time periods for Monday and Tuesday of the same week.

	Monday	Tuesday
0700–0800		
0800–0900		
0900–1000		
1000–1100		
1100–1200		
1200–1300		
1300–1400		
1400–1500		
1500–1600		
1600–1700		
1700–1800		
1800–1900		
1900–2000		
2000–2100		
2100–2200		
2200–2300		
2300–2400		

E X E R C I S E 4.4

STUDY TECHNIQUES FOR THE ACTIVE STUDENT

Indicate, in the response set that follows each hint, the degree to which you apply these aids when studying.

0	1 2 3	4 5 6	7 8 9	10
Never	Seldom	Frequently	Most of the time	Always

1. Set aside a time period of not less than 30 minutes for a review and a minimum of 1 hour for original study.
   Response 0 1 2 3 4 5 6 7 8 9 10

2. Plan your study time in terms of the next day's classes, the day following, and next week.
   Response 0 1 2 3 4 5 6 7 8 9 10

3. Allot sufficient study periods for each course. Allocate 1–2 hours of study time for each hour of in-class time.
   Response 0 1 2 3 4 5 6 7 8 9 10

4. Glance/browse through the entire assignment or reading first and organize it into parts for your study time.
   Response 0 1 2 3 4 5 6 7 8 9 10

5. Read/work/study in segments. You need not accomplish everything at once.
   Response 0 1 2 3 4 5 6 7 8 9 10

6. Highlight, take notes, or develop keywords or other techniques to help you *recall* and *understand* the work later.
   Response 0 1 2 3 4 5 6 7 8 9 10

7. Review your work after you complete it.
   Response 0 1 2 3 4 5 6 7 8 9 10

Interpretation: The higher the score, the more successful you should be as a student. The only qualifier is that when exercising these hints, your total focus must be on studying.

2. Were the study times scheduled complementary to the class time or other study time? That is, was study time set aside and not "squeezed" into a 1-hour break between home and job or between classes? Remember: You can review your notes and work in as short a period as 30 minutes, but original study requires 1-hour blocks.

3. Be sure your study time was not scheduled in conjunction with other activities, such as eating or TV watching (unless, of course, watching a particular program was part of your assignment).

Your New Calendar

In Exercise 4.5, you will complete a new time schedule based on what you have learned about time management in this chapter. Post this and/or carry it with you.

HOW CAN I REALLY CONTROL MY TIME?

This is a very good question, because all of your life you have been taught to be sociable. You have been taught to seek and/or respond to other verbal communications and to be a willing listener when needed. Now it is your turn to take "dedicated time" for yourself *without* feeling guilty. Examine the following five important guidelines for taking control of your time (from David Ellis, *Becoming a Master Student,* 9th ed. and Carol Kanar, *The Confident Student,* 4th ed.).

Use a Regular Study Area

Regardless of whether this location is in a university library, a special place at home, or in a public library, it must be special to you. Every time you are there, you know your focus is study.

Avoid Distractions by Using Background Noise

Many students feel that they cannot study unless they have some form of background noise, such as music. If necessary, you may use instrumental music at a low volume. The purpose is to block out any other outside noises that may filter into your study area. Your "white noise" must not be so explicit as to intrude into your mind with lyrics or lively rhythmic beats.

Be Aware of the Best Time of the Day for You to Study

By this time, you know when you are most physically active, when you are most mentally active, and when it is easiest to sit and concentrate. Utilize this knowledge in the timing of your study periods.

Learn to Say "No"

Time is the only "personal" resource over which you have some control. No one has a right to interrupt you or *demand* your time. You must explain to others that they must respect you and your needs. You will be available to them later. This reflects courtesy on your part and theirs. If they cannot understand this, you may wish to consider limiting your compatriots to those who can respect you.

Don't Procrastinate

Procrastinating is convincing ourselves to put something off to a later time. We are all very good at manufacturing excuses. What we must do is to revise this thought process. We must decide what we can do after completing study assignments, and have this as something to look forward to, rather than looking upon studying as something we can always do later. Exercise 4.7 measures your inclination to procrastinate.

MODERATION

As in all aspects of life, you must take all of your social roles—student, family member, employee, parent—in stride, not permitting any of them to trip you up. This demands moderation. As an adage of the English Church puts it, "Moderation in all things, including moderation." We should seek moderation, or balance, in fulfilling all of our duties, letting no single one dominate us. But at the same time, we should occasionally "splurge" and spend some time just on ourselves.

Now complete the remaining exercises in this chapter.

E X E R C I S E 4.5

YOUR NEW TWO-DAY CALENDAR OF ACTIVITY

Summarize all of your activities during these time periods for Monday and Tuesday of next week. Use extra pages if necessary.

	Monday	Tuesday
0700–0800		
0800–0900		
0900–1000		
1000–1100		
1100–1200		
1200–1300		
1300–1400		
1400–1500		
1500–1600		
1600–1700		
1700–1800		
1800–1900		
1900–2000		
2000–2100		
2100–2200		
2200–2300		
2300–2400		

E X E R C I S E 4.6

TIME MANAGEMENT HINTS FOR THE STUDENT

1. Study environment—a special place dedicated only to study. Describe all the locations you used.

_____

_____

_____

2. Privacy—no interruptions. Describe all the individuals or groups to whom you have made certain hours or meetings off limits.

_____

_____

_____

3. Preparation. Describe all of the materials that you consider appropriate for study and must bring to the study area.

_____

_____

_____

HANG THIS REMINDER IN A PLACE WHERE YOU WILL SEE IT REGULARLY.

E X E R C I S E 4.7

A SELF-TEST OF YOUR "PROCRASTINATION QUOTIENT"

1. I put off doing an assignment if it seems too difficult.
   Strongly Agree _____   Agree _____   Agree Somewhat _____
   Disagree Somewhat _____   Disagree _____   Strongly Disagree _____

2. I put off doing an assignment if completing it will take a lot of time.
   Strongly Agree _____   Agree _____   Agree Somewhat _____
   Disagree Somewhat _____   Disagree _____   Strongly Disagree _____

3. I put off studying if I don't like the subject.
   Strongly Agree _____   Agree _____   Agree Somewhat _____
   Disagree Somewhat _____   Disagree _____   Strongly Disagree _____

4. I put off studying if I'm not in the mood.
   Strongly Agree _____   Agree _____   Agree Somewhat _____
   Disagree Somewhat _____   Disagree _____   Strongly Disagree _____

5. I put off writing an essay if I don't know how to begin.
   Strongly Agree _____   Agree _____   Agree Somewhat _____
   Disagree Somewhat _____   Disagree _____   Strongly Disagree _____

6. I put off studying for a test if I don't know what the test will cover.
   Strongly Agree _____   Agree _____   Agree Somewhat _____
   Disagree Somewhat _____   Disagree _____   Strongly Disagree _____

7. I put off studying if I get hungry.
   Strongly Agree _____   Agree _____   Agree Somewhat _____
   Disagree Somewhat _____   Disagree _____   Strongly Disagree _____

8. I put off studying if I am too tired.
   Strongly Agree _____   Agree _____   Agree Somewhat _____
   Disagree Somewhat _____   Disagree _____   Strongly Disagree _____

9. I put off studying if I don't feel well.
   Strongly Agree _____   Agree _____   Agree Somewhat _____
   Disagree Somewhat _____   Disagree _____   Strongly Disagree _____

10. I put off studying if there is something else I'd rather do.
    Strongly Agree _____   Agree _____   Agree Somewhat _____
    Disagree Somewhat _____   Disagree _____   Strongly Disagree _____

Scoring is as follows:

6	5	4	3	2	1
Strongly Agree	Agree	Agree Somewhat	Disagree Somewhat	Disagree	Strongly Disagree

Obviously, the higher your score, the more you procrastinate and need active remedial work on this area of your student life. A score of over 35 means you need to pay serious attention to this problem area!

C O M P U T E R   E X E R C I S E   4.8

WEB SITES WITH TIME MANAGEMENT IDEAS

Several World Wide Web sites have some references to the topic of time management. Several are listed below. In the space that follows, describe any insights that you derived from these web sites. Remember that most of them include advertisements for books or other publications, which you may wish to find in your local or student library instead of purchasing.

www.selfgrowth.com/timemgt.html (Contains a directory of other web sites.)

www.mindtools.com/lifeplan.html (Search under Mind Tool Resources/Skills for High Performance Living/Time Management Skills.)

www.altavista.com (Search under Time Management Techniques for Students. Again, this is a listing of books that you may or may not wish to buy but can find in a local bookstore or your campus bookstore.)

_____

_____

_____

_____

_____

_____

_____

_____

_____

_____

_____

CHAPTER 5

Successful Learning

Tell me and I will forget;

Show me and I will remember;

Involve me and I will understand.

Chinese Proverb

This simple proverb plainly indicates that successful learning entails *understanding*. This section will focus on the skills that enhance understanding of what you learn.

ADVANCED READING AND NOTE-TAKING SKILLS

If you had learned to fish as a child in the rivers and streams of America and a relative offered to take you deep-sea fishing, you would need to learn new skills of fishing in a different setting. This is similar to learning new reading and note-taking skills when you move from a community college to a four-year university. Your first goal is to understand yourself—that is, to discover your best learning style. This means the approach that you are the most comfortable with and that enables you to acquire information in the shortest amount of time.

First, we will discuss what "sensory preference" you display. That is, through which sense do you most reliably learn? We will discuss three: auditory (hearing), kinesthetic (touch or hands on), and visual (seeing). You may prefer one of these and generally use it more than the others.

In the three sets of exercises that follow, check all of the items that apply to you all the time or most of the time (from R. Hellyer et al., *Study Skills for Learning Power,* 2d ed.).

EXERCISE 5.1

AUDITORY LEARNING

_____ I prefer to have *oral* directions.

_____ Don't show me; tell me.

_____ I need to sound out words (using phonetics) in order to pronounce them.

_____ I like to work in study groups.

_____ I would rather listen to oral reports than read written ones.

_____ I like to interview people or get information by talking to them.

_____ I enjoy the sound of words and like to play word games.

_____ I'm good at remembering jokes or the words to songs, jingles, rhymes, and limericks.

_____ I think it is fairly easy to learn foreign languages.

_____ I learn math best by having someone explain it orally.

THE PHYSICAL SETTING

Studying is more than an activity or even a mental state. It also involves the proper physical setting. You must set aside a particular area in your home to be used *exclusively* for study. If a separate room is not available, then convert an existing area to a study area. If you study in your room, rearrange the furniture when you begin studying. For example, if you have a small table in your room with various items of personal interest, remove these items when you study. Do not allow any distractions in the environment. Then move the table to another location in the room with good light and study there. Do not carry out any other activities with the table in this location. When study time is complete, move the furniture back to its original location.

EXERCISE 5.2

VISUAL LEARNING

____ I prefer to have *written* instructions.

____ Don't tell me; show me.

____ I have to see a word written out to tell if it is spelled correctly.

____ I like to use maps, pictures, and charts.

____ I usually remember where I saw an item in printed material.

____ I prefer to read things for or by myself.

____ I take lots of notes in class and write "to do" lists.

____ I read labels on cans, signs, notices—anything that is available.

____ I notice differences in colors, shapes, and forms.

____ I need to write out math problems, see them written, or use flash cards.

EXERCISE 5.3

"HANDS-ON" LEARNING

____ I prefer *doing* or experimenting with things like computers.

____ I like to manipulate objects physically.

____ I like to spell out words by writing them out.

____ I enjoy handicrafts—cross-stitching, sculpting, building models, etc.

____ I am mechanically inclined.

____ I find texture to be important in decorating or selecting clothing.

____ I like to "talk with my hands."

____ I enjoy being physically active (I don't like to sit still).

____ If I am learning something, I need to "walk through" the steps.

____ I like to learn by using contour maps, scientific models, or other touchable materials.

u must advise your family and friends that during this preplanned time pe-
d, you do not perform other tasks, such as caring for siblings; reading sto-
; performing household chores; or even answering pages, cell phone calls,
 egular phone calls. Neither will you have the television or other visual dis-
tions in your vicinity.

 ou may have light music as background. The music should not have lyrics,
and the sound level must be low. It should be considered as "white noise," the
background sound needed to muffle the outside noises that may filter through
the walls or closed door to your room.

Mentally prepare yourself for study by asking yourself, "What am I going to
learn today?" This is your preparatory mental state when you sit down. Now
you are ready to study.

ADVANCED READING TECHNIQUES

Surveying Your Textbook

After carefully reading your course syllabus (the document given to you by
your instructor at the beginning of the academic term that details the "references" or "reference readings" designated for segments of classroom presentation), bring *all* the textbooks for the course together and survey them in
accordance with the syllabus outline.

Begin your reading of any textbook with both the "brief table of contents"
(if one appears) and the general table of contents. Include the author's introduction, because it will explain the order in which the author has chosen to
present the information and will give you valuable information about his or
her approach to the material.

> Example:
> *Brief Contents*
> Chapter 4   Social Structure and Social Interaction
> *General Contents*
> Chapter 4   Social Structure and Social Interaction
> Section 4.1   The Micro-sociological Perspective:
>   Social Interaction in Everyday Life
>   Symbolic Interaction
>   Dramaturgy: The Presentation of Self in Everyday Life

Reading "from the Outside in"

After correlating the course syllabus with the textbook and understanding the
author's organizational style, begin your reading "from the outside in." Most
textbooks are organized by substantive sections (i.e., culture, vertebrate tax-

onomy, quadratic equations, etc.), so you should focus your attention on the subject of the section and read all of the subsection and sub-subsection titles. You can usually recognize the different levels of titles by their distinctive colors or by their different typefaces or styles (bold or italic).

After surveying the order in which the topics are presented in the textbook, compare this with the instructor's syllabus, because many instructors do not follow the order shown in the textbook. You are now ready to begin your reading of the materials on which your instructor will lecture.

Writing in Your Textbook (It's Okay!)

Note taking is a shorthand method of setting up a pattern of mental recall. It is all right to highlight phrases or section titles in your textbook—and even to write in the margins. However, these notes should not be complete sentences unless they are technical definitions. Why? When you review the textbook, these notes should be for recall, *not* re-reading. Re-reading notes does not accomplish the intended purpose unless you are prepared to re-read them many times and commit them to memory.

Given that our goal is understanding (remember that Chinese proverb at the beginning of the chapter), recall is a higher level of knowledge and requires understanding of the broader context of the information.

It is also important to remember that one reads at different rates, depending on the content of the material. A fast reader is NOT NECESSARILY a good student, nor is a slow reader necessarily a bad student. The speed of reading is not relevant; comprehension (understanding) is.

Reading Supplemental Materials

Most instructors provide supplemental reading lists for students. Some of these lists are required reading and are available at your library's Reserve Desk. Or your instructor may place them on the Internet at a particular web site. In any case, they are materials that are relevant to the subject under discussion in the course and that "flesh out" what the instructor can present in the classroom period.

If the instructor does not give you a supplemental reading list, then check the Bibliography or Reference section of your text, either at the end of each chapter or at the end of the book. These may be particularly helpful if you did not quite understand the instructor or the textbook material.

ADVANCED NOTE-TAKING TECHNIQUES

Taking Notes in Lectures and Seminars

Different techniques are used to incorporate material from lectures (or readings) into one's notes for later recall. Two common methods are the clustering

Figure 5.1
The clustering method of note taking

Source: Carol Kanar, *The Confident Student,* Fourth Edition. Copyright © 2001 by Houghton Mifflin Company. Reprinted with permission.

method (Figure 5.1) and the Cornell method (Figure 5.2). Both of these methods employ the technique of "mind mapping." The student is more free to return and add supplementary notes.

Figures 5.3 and 5.4 are examples of other approaches: highlighting and underlining, respectively. Underlining is obviously a technique to use with written material. Highlighting works with both lectures and reading assignments.

Literature 2010   Sept. 18

	The five elements of Fiction
	1. Plot
How does the	a. Events and setting
plot of the	b. Plot development
story develop?	• conflict
	• complications
	• climax
	• resolution
	2. Character
What is the	a. Dynamic
difference between	• well-rounded
a dynamic and a	• motives
static character?	b. Static
	• flat
	• stereotype
	3. Point of view
What are the	a. First person
four points	b. Omniscient
of view?	c. Limited omniscient
	d. Dramatic
How is the	4. Theme
theme of the	a. Meaning or significance
story revealed?	b. Revealed through interaction of five elements
What makes one	5. Style/Tone
writer's style	a. Mood or feeling
distinctive?	b. Choice of words, use of language

The writer uses five elements of fiction—plot, character, point of view, theme, and style/tone—to develop the story. Through the interaction of these elements, the meaning of the story is revealed and the reader can understand its significance.

Figure 5.2
The Cornell method of note taking

Source: Carol Kanar, *The Confident Student*, Fourth Edition. Copyright © 2001 by Houghton Mifflin Company. Reprinted with permission.

Units of Analysis

In social scientific research, there is virtually no limit to what or whom can be studied, or the **units of analysis.** This topic is relevant to all forms of social research, although its implications are clearest in the case of nomothetic, quantitative studies.

Social scientists perhaps most typically choose individual people as their units of analysis. You may note the characteristics of individual people—gender, age, region of birth, attitudes, and so forth. You can then combine these descriptions to provide a composite picture of the group the individuals represent, whether a street-corner gang or a whole society.

For example, you may note the age and gender of each student enrolled in Political Science 110 and then characterize the group of students as being 53 percent men and 47 percent women and as having a mean age of 18.6 years, or a descriptive analysis. Although the final description would be of the class as a whole, the individual characteristics are aggregated for purposes of describing some larger group.

The same aggregation would occur in an explanatory study. Suppose you wished to discover whether students with a high grade point average received better grades in Political Science 110 than did students with a low GPA. You would measure the GPAs and the course grades of individual students. You might then aggregate students with a high GPA and those with a low GPA and see which group received the best grades in the course. The purpose of the study would be to explain why some students do better in the course than others (looking at overall grade point averages as a possible explanation), but individual students would still be the units of analysis.

Units of analysis in a study are typically also the units of observation. Thus, to study voting intentions, we would interview ("observe") individual voters. Sometimes, however, we "observe" our units of analysis indirectly. For example, we might ask husbands and wives their individual voting intentions, for the purpose of distinguishing couples who agree and disagree politically. We might want to find out whether

political disagreements tend to cause divorce, perhaps. In this case, our units of analysis would be families, though the units of observation would be the individual wives and husbands.

Units of analysis, then, are those things we examine in order to create summary descriptions of all such units and to explain differences among them. This concept should be clarified further as we now consider several common social science units of analysis.

Individuals

As mentioned previously, individual human beings are perhaps the most typical units of analysis for social scientific research. We tend to describe and explain social groups and interactions by aggregating and manipulating the descriptions of individuals.

Any type of individual may be the unit of analysis for social scientific research. This point is more important than it may seem at first reading. The norm of *generalized understanding* in social science should suggest that scientific findings are most valuable when they apply to *all* kinds of people. In practice, however, social scientists seldom study all kinds of people. At the very least, their studies are typically limited to the people living in a single country, though some comparative studies stretch across national boundaries. Often, though, studies are quite circumscribed.

Examples of specific groups whose members may be units of analysis—at the individual level—include students, gays and lesbians, auto workers, voters, single parents, and faculty members. Note that each of these terms implies some population of individual persons. (See chapter 8 for more on populations.) At this point, it's enough to realize that descriptive studies with individuals as their units of analysis typically aim to describe the population that comprises those individuals, whereas explanatory studies aim to discover the social dynamics operating within that population.

As the units of analysis, individuals may be characterized in terms of their membership in social groupings. Thus, an individual may be described as belonging to a rich family or to a poor one, or a person may be described as having a college-educated mother or not. We might examine in a research project whether people with college-educated mothers are more likely

Figure 5.3

An example of note taking

Source: Earl Babbie, *The Basics of Social Research* (Belmont, CA: Wadsworth Publishing, 1999), page 75.

to attend college than those with non-college-educated mothers or whether high school graduates in rich families are more likely to attend college than those in poor families. In each case, the individual would be the unit of analysis—not the mother or the family.

Groups

Social groups themselves may also be the units of analysis for social scientific research. Realize how this differs from studying the individuals within a group. If you were to study the members of a criminal gang to learn about criminals, for example, the individual (criminal) would be the unit of analysis; but if you studied all the gangs in a city to learn the differences, say, between big gangs and small ones, between "uptown" and "downtown" gangs, and so forth, the unit of analysis would be the *gang*, a social group.

Here's another example. You might describe families in terms of total annual income and according to whether or not they had computers. You could aggregate families and describe the mean income of families and the percentage with computers. You would then be in a position to determine whether families with higher incomes were more likely to have computers than those with lower incomes. The individual family in such a case would be the unit of analysis.

Other units of analysis at the groups level could be friendship cliques, married couples, census blocks, cities, or geographic regions. Each of these terms also implies some population. *Street gangs* implies some population that includes all street gangs. The population of street gangs could be be described, say, in terms of its geographical distribution throughout a city, and an explanatory study of street gangs might discover, say, whether large gangs were more likely than small ones to engage in intergang warfare.

Organizations

Formal social organizations may also be the units of analysis in social scientific research. An example would be corporations, implying, of course, a population of all corporations. Individual corporations might be characterized in terms of their number of employees, net annual profits, gross assets, number of defense contracts, percentage of employees from racial or ethnic minority groups, and so forth. We might determine whether large corporations hire a larger or smaller percentage of minority group employees than small corporations. Other examples of formal social organizations suitable as units of analysis would be church congregations, colleges, army divisions, academic departments, and supermarkets.

As with other units of analysis, we can derive the characteristics of social groups from those of their individual members. Thus, we might describe a family in terms of the age, race, or education of its head. In a descriptive study, then, we might find the percentage of all families that have a college-educated head of family. In an explanatory study, we might determine whether such families have, on the average, more or fewer children than families headed by people who have not graduated from college. In each of these examples, however, the *family* would be the unit of analysis. Had we asked whether college graduates—college-educated *individuals*—have more or fewer children than their less educated counterparts, then the individual person would have been the unit of analysis.

Social groups may be characterized in other ways, such as according to their environments or their membership in larger groupings. Families, for example, might be described in terms of their dwelling. We might want to determine whether rich families are more likely to reside in single-family houses (as opposed to, say, apartments) than poor families. The unit of analysis would still be the family.

If all this seems unduly complicated, be assured that in most research projects you are likely to undertake, the unit of analysis will be relatively clear to you. When the unit of analysis is not so clear, however, it is absolutely essential to determine what it is; otherwise, you cannot determine what observations are to be made about whom or what.

Some studies try to describe or explain more than one unit of analysis. In these cases, the researcher must anticipate what conclusions she or he wishes to draw with regard to which units of analysis.

Figure 5.4
Another example of note taking

Source: Earl Babbie, *The Basics of Social Research* (Belmont, CA: Wadsworth Publishing, 1999), page 76.

It is important to recognize that none of these approaches is always "correct." Each is "correct" only if it helps the student learner to recall, at a later time, information presented or read with understanding.

As important as these physical techniques are, it is also important to realize that you are an active learner and that the way in which you listen to oral presentations affects your note taking, comprehension, and recall. Examine this for yourself in the following exercise.

E X E R C I S E 5.4

LISTENING SURVEY

Check the answers that best describe your behaviors and attitudes in your *least* interesting class. (From Hellyer et al., *Study Skills for Learning Power,* 2d ed.)

	Always	Usually	Sometimes	Never
1. I arrive at class on time.	____	____	____	____
2. I have my homework completed.	____	____	____	____
3. I take lots of notes.	____	____	____	____
4. I look out the window.	____	____	____	____
5. I am distracted by other students.	____	____	____	____
6. My mind wanders in class.	____	____	____	____
7. I expect the teacher to be entertaining.	____	____	____	____
8. I work on homework for other classes in this class.	____	____	____	____
9. I think using a tape recorder is just as good as taking notes.	____	____	____	____
10. I sit in the front row.	____	____	____	____

According to Hellyer et al., if you answered questions 1, 2, 3, and 10 with "Always" or "Usually" and questions 4 through 9 with "Sometimes" or "Never," you are a power learner. If not, you may need to reexamine your attitudes and behaviors related to your classes before you step into the classroom. In other words, get "psyched up" for the class and look forward to what you are going to learn.

Note Taking from Written Material

Much of your note taking will be from prepared written material, such as textbooks and assigned readings. In the following exercise, we will examine the techniques that you employ to find the key words or phrases in the written material and the notation system you utilize to recall the information. Remember, underlining or highlighting entire sentences requires you to re-read the material, not recall it. Therefore, your notation system should be geared to words or short phrases that will stimulate your recall of the information. Direct note taking in your textbook is illustrated in Figures 5.3 and 5.4. On the following pages, we describe an alternative method of recording information at the time of first reading for later correlation with your in-class notes.

Your assignment is to read the professional commentary in Exercise 5.5 and make notes on this document as you would in your text or other reading material on which you expect to be examined (tested) later.

E X E R C I S E 5.5

NOTE TAKING FROM WRITTEN MATERIAL

ATTITUDES VERSUS PERSPECTIVES

Perspectives are different from attitudes. When we use the term *perspective* to describe the human being, we enter the world of definition. When we use the term *attitude,* we enter the world of response. This is why symbolic interactionism is an examination of perspectives and reference groups, whereas traditional social psychology is an examination of attitudes and social influence. The distinction here is subtle, but very important.

To focus on attitude is to focus on the individual, because an attitude is part of the individual. It is similar to a trait that is developed socially but carried around from situation to situation. An attitude is an internal response to an object or class of objects. The external environment acts as a stimulus; the person responds internally. Then the person responds externally following that internal response. When we have an attitude toward other people who are women or African Americans or poets, and an individual in one of these categories enters our presence, our attitude is thought to be activated, leading us to act in a certain direction. The attitude is a predisposition; it predisposes us to act a certain way. The actor is not thought to be in charge of his or her own action; the actor does not use the attitude, but instead, the attitude directs the actor. To use the term *attitude* is to describe the human being as a passive being and to ignore the importance of active definition of the situation.

A perspective, on the other hand, is not a response to a stimulus but something used as a guide to definition. It is not an internal trait but something belonging to, arising in, shared in, and changing in social interaction. The individual uses it; it does not cause behavior. Because the individual interacts with many others and exists in many social worlds, he or she will have many perspectives, and therefore, no given object is a simple stimulus. Rather, it can be defined in a number of ways, depending on the actor's goals in the situation. A person I see in a situation may be Chinese, a teacher, a male, an artist, a scholar, a liberal, and a member of the upper class, but whatever I focus on and how I decide to act will depend on how I define him or her in the situation; and my definition, in turn, will be influenced by the perspective I use to define the situation. Any one of the individual's characteristics may or may not be important to me. For example, although I may be prejudiced against artists (an attitude), that may or may not be an important influence on my action, because I am seeing the individual as a teacher in the perspective that I am using.

An attitude is usually defined as a quality of the individual, so it is thought to be fairly fixed and stable over time. An attitude is generally seen to be tied to other qualities of the person, including other attitudes. The image of the human being described is one of a consistent, whole organism responding to stimuli in situations according to this attitude brought to the situation. "He has an attitude toward women that causes him to treat them as property whenever he encounters them." Perspectives, on the other hand, are conceptualized as dynamic and changing, guides to interpretation and then to action, undergoing change during the interaction and not necessarily consistent within the actor.

Action can therefore never be perfectly predictable. Even if we know the perspectives an actor carries into a situation, we do not know beforehand which one will be chosen by the actor, nor can we predict how it will change in that situation. And even if we know the perspective that will be used, we still cannot know exactly how the individual will use it to define the situation. Finally, we must also recognize that whatever perspectives the actor brings to a situation may, over time, be put aside in favor of one that arises in the actual situation. The selection of juries that favor our side in a courtroom will depend on knowing what groups they interact with on an ongoing basis, and therefore which perspectives they might use to define the trial, but it is central to recognize that the perspective that emerges from the interaction of the jurors may become the most important one by far. Knowing the attitude an individual may have, according to symbolic interactionism, will give us much less information about how the jury member will vote.

Clearly, a different type of actor is conceptualized when we use the concept *perspective* rather than *attitude*. Human beings interact, use perspectives, define situations, act according to their present time interpretation, and are active and dynamic actors.

Evaluation

How many phrases and definitions within the text did you highlight or underline?_____

How many words or short phrases did you write in the margins?_____

Did you write your notes on a separate page of paper? If yes, how did you organize them?_____

_____

Now, to analyze your own note-taking skills, answer the following questions *without* referring to your notes. This is not a test of factual retention but, rather, an exercise to help you understand how different note-taking techniques lead to different outcomes in the testing or examination phase of instruction.

True/False

1. _____ An attitude is usually defined as an attribute of the individual.

2. _____ A perspective is a response to a stimulus.

3. _____ Human beings interact and use perspectives.

4. _____ The actor does not use an attitude, but the attitude directs the actor.

5. _____ Perspectives are dynamic and changing.

Fill in the Blank

6. An attitude is usually defined as _____

_____.

7. Perspectives are conceptualized as _____

_____.

8. An interaction utilizes a _____
and arrives at a perspective.

Short Answer

Describe the difference between an attitude and a perspective, according to the author, and give an example of each.

_____

_____

_____

_____

_____

_____

ADVANCED RESEARCH TECHNIQUES

Bibliographic and Cited References

As you progress in your academic career, you will be reading many professional journal articles and books. A *complete* reading of any such assignment includes the Bibliography or Cited References at the end of the assignment. These are lists of the materials accessed by the authors who prepared the article or book you are reading. Many additional sources may be found, to elaborate your search for further information, by referring to these two sources.

Computer Searches

Databases

Your search in the various databases of your library's computerized system, if available, will generate additional references for your review. Some of the most common databases are OCLC, OPAC, CARL, and Lexis-Nexis.

C O M P U T E R   E X E R C I S E 5.6

COMPUTER SEARCH ON YOUR CAMPUS

List all of the databases you most commonly use for your academic work, as well as the web sites, if required. Reference them by topic or course number.

Topic or Course Number	Database	Web Site Address

The search of abstracts, which are summaries of (1) professional journal articles, (2) papers presented at professional meetings, and (3) dissertations for your academic discipline, will provide you with a vast array of other resources to supplement your assigned materials.

Each academic discipline has a computerized set of abstracts. You may print out these abstracts directly (at some campuses) or store them on a diskette to be printed out later or write down the necessary information from the line that reads "JOURNAL" on the page where the abstract appears.

Linked Terms

At the bottom of each abstract page is a list of "linked terms," which are the computer search terms by which you may also access the same subject.

JSTOR

On some campuses with a computerized library system, you may print out the actual article for which you are searching by using the abbreviation JSTOR, which refers to a journal storage and retrieval system. You should check with your reference librarian to ensure you have access and to become familiar with the method of retrieval required on that campus.

Critique Your Note Taking Using the Bloom Taxonomy

An educator by the name of Bloom devised a taxonomy for teachers and students using key words in the English language to measure different levels of understanding. The categories progress from the simple recall of information through the ability to evaluate the material studied.

For Exercise 5.7, review the reading from Exercise 5.5. With what you can recollect from the reading and using Bloom's levels of understanding, complete Exercise 5.7 following the instructions provided with the exercise. Why do this? These are the standard types of questions that are asked in examinations to have you, the student, *reflect* back on your reading and *recall* either information or an interpretive understanding of what you have read.

Interpretation

Take note of the verbs in Exercise 5.7 where you were able to readily identify the action or response. Review the same passage again and repeat the exercise, completing the unanswered verbs from your first attempt. In this way, you will have a greater mastery of the subject matter and be able to express that knowledge in multiple formats if asked.

E X E R C I S E 5.7

CRITIQUE YOUR NOTE TAKING: THE BLOOM TAXONOMY

Using your reading of the article "Attitudes Versus Perspectives" in Exercise 5.5, examine how many of the levels of understanding in the Bloom taxonomy you have mastered. For example, if you know the definitions for the terms *attitude* and *perspective*, write the words *attitude* and *perspective* on the DEFINE line. (From Benjamin Bloom, *Taxonomy of Educational Objectives: The Classification of Educational Goals*.)

Level 1 KNOWLEDGE
The recall of information

DEFINE _____

DESCRIBE _____

LIST _____

MATCH _____

RECOGNIZE _____

RECALL _____

Level 2 COMPREHENSION
The translation, interpretation, or extrapolation of knowledge

ARRANGE _____

CLASSIFY _____

EXPLAIN _____

LOCATE _____

REPORT _____

IDENTIFY _____

Level 3 APPLICATION
The application of knowledge to a new situation

APPLY _____

CHOOSE _____

ILLUSTRATE _____

DEMONSTRATE _____

SOLVE _____

PRACTICE _____

Level 4   ANALYSIS
Breaking down knowledge into parts and showing relationships among the parts

ANALYZE _____

CONTRAST _____

DIFFERENTIATE _____

COMPARE _____

CRITICIZE _____

DIAGRAM _____

Level 5   SYNTHESIS
Bringing together parts (elements and components) of knowledge to form a whole and building relationships for new situations

ARRANGE _____

DESIGN _____

SET UP _____

SYNTHESIZE _____

CREATE _____

PLAN _____

Level 6   EVALUATION
Making judgments about the value of material and methods for given purposes

APPRAISE _____

SUPPORT _____

DEFEND _____

JUDGE _____

ASSESS _____

EVALUATE _____

In the following space, use a common concept (such as gender or another) for which you have developed an explanatory narrative previously. Now choose another verb and rewrite the same concept. At the conclusion, you should have a better understanding of both the concept and your ability to communicate it.

_____

_____

_____

_____

_____

_____

_____

_____

So What Do All These Exercises Mean?

What you have learned in this chapter are advanced techniques to enhance your understanding of the materials you are studying, as well as selected techniques for best utilizing existing resources on your campus, in computerized library files and with reference librarians, and in the bibliographies that appear in your assignments themselves. A combination of these skills will result in better comprehension, more self-confidence, greater knowledge, and better grades.

CHAPTER 6

Higher-Order Thinking: Becoming a Critical Thinker

One of the goals of the university is to move students from lower-order thinking to higher-order thinking. What, then, is the difference between lower-order and higher-order thinking?

Lower-order thinking refers to a limited, superficial, and unsophisticated way of thinking about and understanding the world. When you are engaged in lower-order thinking, you are not utilizing your evaluative and analytical skills. Memorizing information and then restating it on a test is an example of lower-order thinking. The exam is testing your ability to memorize and is not necessarily measuring your understanding of the material.

Higher-order thinking is the ability to analyze information using specific skills that enable you to shed light on the issue at hand. Often referred to as "critical thinking," this way of looking at information extends beyond the classroom. It could and should be used in analyzing and understanding all aspects of your life: academics, health, politics, personal relationships, and work.

In college you will have the occasional professor whose teaching technique evokes only lower-order thinking. In these classes, tests typically ask you to regurgitate what the professor recited in class during lectures. Students are not required to critique, to integrate, or to analyze. You might think this is a great type of class to have and be tempted to enroll in as many of these classes as possible. But be careful! You would be cheating yourself of the opportunity to hone very important skills that you will need to be successful in life, work, and relationships with others.

ELEMENTS OF CRITICAL THINKING

Critical thinking encompasses skills and tools that help you engage in higher-order thinking. The Center for Critical Thinking at Sonoma State University believes the concept of critical thinking is rather simple: It is "the art of taking charge of your own mind." To think critically is to use careful judgment and evaluation. Most of us need to be schooled or trained on how to take charge of our own minds and on how to employ careful judgment and evaluation. In fact, many colleges require a critical thinking course as part of its general education requirements.

This chapter will cover the important elements of critical thinking: systems of reasoning, differentiating between fact and opinion, common pitfalls that may stand in the way of logical thinking, and the evaluation of information sources.

SYSTEMS OF LOGICAL REASONING

Whether or not you realize it, you go through life and your daily activities explaining things. Of course, in your academic work, you are often asked to explain historical events, scientific results, human behavior, and the like. But even apart from your academic assignments, to navigate successfully in your world, you are regularly engaged in explaining your environment and your actions to yourself and others.

Here are some examples. Let's suppose you're having a really bad hair day. As you catch a scary glimpse of yourself and see your hair all out of control, you may try to figure out what caused this calamity. Was it the new shampoo you used that morning? The humid weather? Or maybe you were running late that morning and didn't have time to wash and style your hair. Now substitute a situation from your academic life. You just aced that chemistry quiz! This is the first A you have received in that course. How would you explain that? Did you study more or differently for this quiz? Maybe this quiz was much easier than the previous ones. Seeking answers to questions and problems, or trying to explain phenomena, is something you do all day long.

Generally, there are two main ways in which we reason and explain events such as a bad hair day or doing well on an exam. These two systems of reasoning are called inductive and deductive logic.

Inductive Reasoning

In his book *The Practice of Social Research*, Earl Babbie, a sociologist, describes inductive reasoning by presenting the following scenario. (From *The Practice of Social Research with InfoTrac*, 9th ed. by E. Babbie. Copyright © 2001. Reprinted with permission of Wadsworth, an imprint of the Wadsworth Group, a division of Thomson Learning. Fax 800-730-2215.)

> You might find yourself puzzling, halfway through your college career, why you do so well on exams sometimes but poorly at other times. You might list all the exams you've taken, noting how well you did on each. Then you might try to recall any circumstances shared by all the good exams and by all the poor ones. Did you do better on multiple-choice exams or essay exams? Morning exams or afternoon exams? Exams in the natural sciences, the humanities, or the social sciences? Times when you studied alone or . . . SHAZAM! It occurs to you that you have almost always done best on ex-

ams when you studied with others. This mode of inquiry is known as **induction.** Inductive reasoning moves from the particular to the general, from a set of specific observations to the discovery of a pattern that represents some degree of order among all the given events. (Babbie, 1998:35)

By analyzing your performance on all your exams (specific observations), you have discovered that you perform best on exams when you study with others (a pattern that all the events exhibit). From looking at the particulars (exam performance), you have *induced* a general pattern (study groups work well for you).

Deductive Reasoning

Now, using the same theme of exam performance, this is how Earl Babbie describes the other system of reasoning: deductive logic.

Here's a very different way you might have arrived at the same conclusion about studying for exams. Imagine approaching your first set of exams in college. You wonder about the best ways to study—how much you should review the readings, how much you should focus on your class notes. You learn that some students prepare by rewriting their notes in an orderly fashion. Then you consider if you should study at a measured pace or else pull an all-nighter just before the exam. Among these kinds of musings, you might ask whether you should get together with other students in the class or just study on your own. You could evaluate the pros and cons of both options. . . . You might add up the pros and cons and conclude, logically, that you'd benefit from studying with others. It seems reasonable to you, the way it seems reasonable that you'll do better if you study rather than not. Sometimes, we say things like this are true "in theory." To complete the process, we test whether they are true in practice. For a complete test, you might study alone for half your exams and study with others for the other exams. This procedure would test your logical reasoning. This second mode of inquiry is known as **deduction.** (Babbie, 1998:36)

With deductive reasoning, you move from the general to the specific. The general principles in this example were some thoughts, beliefs, or theories about studying alone versus studying with others. The specific aspect is the act of studying with others and observing whether your test performance improves.

You may ask, "Why is this important to know and how is it related to my course work?" As Walter Pauk explains in his book *How to Study in College*, the ability to tell whether your instructors and readings are using deductive or inductive reasoning will enhance your understanding of the material. An inductive pattern exists when the instructor "identifies a number of incidents and draws a conclusion from them. The speaker's main point will be something like this: 'So, on the basis of all these facts, we come to this overriding principle, which is so-and-so' (Pauk, 1997:180). With a deductive pattern, the instructor makes a general statement and then lists the events or proofs. If you understand that course material and information can be presented in different ways and you are able to identify whether the presenter is using deductive or inductive logic, it will help you in note taking, in reading, and in writing reports and research papers.

EVALUATING ARGUMENTS AND CLAIMS

Earlier in this chapter, we said that to think critically means to use careful judgment and evaluation. In and out of school, you will be confronted with arguments, claims, and statements about how the world operates. It is your responsibility as a critical thinker to be able to judge the soundness of those statements. By carefully judging and evaluating a statement, you can determine whether it is merely someone's opinion or a fact. When confronted with an argument or simple statements containing numerous claims, you have three options. You can (1) accept the claims as being true, (2) reject the claims as being false, or (3) reserve judgment so you can investigate the claims further. The third option is often the most judicious strategy, especially if you are not well versed on the subject matter. A critical thinker is comfortable stating that he or she doesn't know and needs to look into the matter.

You may wonder why it is important to know whether claims made are based on fact or are purely someone's opinion. The answer is that one can *prove* the truth of a fact-based statement, whereas opinion-based statements are just that, someone's belief or preference. Often, beliefs and opinions are based on incorrect or misleading information. During the course of your college experience and throughout your adult life, you will be required to take positions on a variety of topics and present evidence in support of your position. Whether you are asked to do this in the form of a library research paper, for an essay on an exam, or in a class presentation, your instructors will be looking for factual arguments, not opinions or feelings.

Outside school, in your nonacademic life, you will need to make informed decisions on a variety of topics and issues. You may have multiple job offers and need to determine which is best for you, or you may have to purchase a car and need to wade through various persuasive sales pitches to arrive at an informed decision. And, what about deciding which vitamins to take or which weight-loss program is medically sound? To say nothing of the ever-important civic duty of exercising your right to vote and making choices between competing candidates and issues! All of these examples involve individuals making claims in an attempt to persuade you to behave in a certain manner.

Critical thinkers have the skills necessary to cut through the arguments and to determine what is fact and what is solely someone's opinion. Supporting your position with feelings, emotions, and opinions is antithetical to critical thinking and could have disastrous effects on your academic and personal lives. Important decisions should be made on the basis of one's evaluation of the facts pertinent to the issue at hand.

E X E R C I S E 6.1

INDUCTIVE AND DEDUCTIVE REASONING

From your personal or academic life, provide an example of deductive reasoning and an example of inductive reasoning. You might want to review class notes or assigned readings for examples of these reasoning systems. Or you could think about occurrences in your everyday life and identify situations wherein you use inductive and/or deductive reasoning.

> Example: You're sitting in the park near a playground and observe children playing. You notice that for the children over 6 years of age, the boys play only with other boys and the girls play only with other girls. However, with the younger children, boys and girls interact with each other. You might conclude that very young children are not cognizant of sex differences and are comfortable interacting with everyone, whereas older children are aware of gender differences and prefer interacting with members of the same sex. This is an example of inductive reasoning: going from observations to a generalization.

1. Provide a detailed account of deductive reasoning found in your course work or based on your personal experience. First, state a theory or claim. Then describe your specific application of that principle and cite the evidence, events, and proofs to support the claim.

_____

_____

_____

_____

_____

_____

_____

_____

_____

_____

_____

2. Provide a detailed account of inductive reasoning found in your course work or based on your personal experience. First, describe the events, incidents, and evidence. Then state the conclusion you base on these proofs.

_____

_____

_____

_____

_____

_____

_____

_____

_____

_____

_____

Systems of Evidence: Fact Versus Opinion

How, then, can you tell the difference between a factual/empirical statement and an opinion-based statement? Here are some guidelines, adapted from Urquidi's Normative-Empirical Differentiation Test. *Fact-based statements* are

Objective in that they describe what "is" rather than what "ought" to be

Provable/testable

Measurable/quantifiable

Tangible/verifiable

Able to be proved true or false

Opinion-based statements, by contrast, may be

A reflection of personal values

Preferences/recommendations: what we "ought" to do

Beliefs/assumptions

Opinions/attitudes

Predictions/forecasts/speculations/hunches

Here are some examples of fact-based and opinion-based statements:

"Women vote more than men." This is a fact-based statement because it is describing something that "is." It is testable: All we need do is review voting statistics to see whether, in fact, women do indeed vote at higher rates than men. Thus this statement can be proved true or false. However, be aware that fact-based statements are not always true. What differentiates a fact-based statement from an opinion is that the truth or falsity of a fact-based statement can be determined. Even though the statement "Men vote more than women" is false, it would be considered fact-based because the veracity of the statement can be tested.

"Welfare recipients should be made to work." This is an opinion-based statement because it is stating someone's belief about what "ought" to be done. It reflects someone's desires/preferences, and it is really someone's opinion about welfare policy. This statement is not testable, nor can it be proved true or false. Compare this statement to the following statement: "Welfare-to-work programs have been successful in many states." This is an example of a fact-based statement. Why? Because you can research the success of such programs in states throughout the country to determine whether the statement is true or false.

Fallacious Reasoning: Common Pitfalls on the Way to Logical Reasoning

The *Compact American Dictionary* defines *fallacious* as "tending to mislead; deceptive" (1998: 304). Many of us engage in fallacious reasoning without realizing it. Six common fallacies will be discussed in this section.

Wishful thinking and **denial** are types of unsound reasoning. Wishful thinking and denial occur when we block out unpleasant realities and refuse to see things and events clearly. People who have graduated from a couple of alcoholic drinks to weekends of binge drinking may try to excuse this behavior by telling themselves it is harmless fun or innocent entertainment. The reality is the behavior is dangerous. The individual is in denial and is refusing to see things clearly.

On a less serious note, we all know of people who buy lottery tickets. The odds of winning are infinitesimal. Yet they are eternally hopeful that they have the winning ticket. Wishful thinking strikes again!

Common practice is a fallacious argument in which one attempts to justify certain behaviors or beliefs by claiming they are commonly practiced. Some people fudge a little on their income tax returns, arguing that everyone cheats a little. This claim of cheating as a common practice is used to justify unlawful behavior. But the fact that many people engage in unlawful behaviors does not make it right. A critical thinker would reject any claim or argument based solely on the justification that it is a common practice.

Emotional or emotive arguments and words are often used to persuade. You need to identify emotionally charged words and symbols, get past them, and try to uncover the facts. The product ad suggesting that not buying your

E X E R C I S E 6.2

FACT-BASED AND OPINION-BASED STATEMENTS

Part A

Indicate whether each of the following statements is fact-based (F) or opinion-based (O). (From Donald Urquidi, *Decoding Media Messages II.*)

_____ 1. The United States has an obligation to provide economic assistance to underdeveloped countries.

_____ 2. On the whole, African-Americans in the United States are financially better off today than they were ten years ago.

_____ 3. Labor unions have far too much power over the country.

_____ 4. Of all recent presidents, President Kennedy was the best.

_____ 5. Of all recent presidents, President Kennedy was the most well-liked.

_____ 6. The death penalty is barbaric and should be permanently abolished.

_____ 7. The rich should be taxed heavily.

_____ 8. Men and women have a right to find out, before marriage, whether they are sexually compatible.

_____ 9. More men believe than women that couples have a right to find out, before marriage, whether they are sexually compatible.

_____ 10. Jews tend to support the Democratic Party, whereas most Protestants tend to support the Republican Party.

_____ 11. People 18 to 24 years old have the lowest voting turnout rate of any age group.

_____ 12. Roses are prettier than carnations.

_____ 13. Americans ought to exercise at least three times a week.

_____ 14. Exercising at least three times per week reduces the risk of heart disease.

_____ 15. Dogs make better pets than cats.

Answers to this exercise can be found on the next page.

Part B

Select a current newspaper story from a reputable newspaper (*The National Enquirer, The Star,* and other supermarket tabloids do not fall into this category). Read the article and determine which statements are fact-based and which are opinion-based. (Do not select an opinion piece; these are usually identified as editorials, op-ed pieces, or commentaries.)

1. Write down examples of opinion-based statements.

_____

_____

_____

_____

2. Write down examples of fact-based statements.

_____

_____

_____

_____

3. Does the story lead you to draw certain conclusions? If yes, what conclusion would you draw and why? Is this conclusion based mostly on factual statements or on opinion-based statements? Provide examples.

_____

_____

_____

_____

Answers to Exercise 6.2: 1. Opinion, 2. Fact, 3. Opinion, 4. Opinion, 5. Fact, 6. Opinion, 7. Opinion, 8. Opinion, 9. Fact, 10. Fact, 11. Fact, 12. Opinion, 13. Opinion, 14. Fact, 15. Opinion

beloved an expensive ring signifies that you don't love him or her is toying with your emotions. Likewise, politicians who "wrap themselves in the American flag" and refuse to discuss important issues are playing on our patriotic emotions. Once you understand how you are being manipulated by emotional appeals, you are on your way to becoming a critical thinker.

Ad hominem **attacks** are used, often successfully, to divert attention away from the facts of the matter by engaging in name calling. A famous and rather funny *ad hominem* attack took place on the floor of the U.S. Senate in the 1970s. Senators were debating the proposed Equal Rights Amendment (which eventually narrowly failed to pass). One particular senator walked to the podium and stated that those who supported the Equal Rights Amendment were just a "band of braless bubbleheads." Rather than engaging in serious debate based on the facts relevant to the issue, this senator resorted to name calling.

False dilemma is a common fallacy. Whenever you are presented with only two choices, when in reality there are more than two choices, you are confronting a false dilemma. During the 1960s a famous slogan used against students protesting the Vietnam War was "America: Love It or Leave It." The false dilemma is that only two options are given: Love your country (and don't exercise your constitutional right to protest) or leave your country and live elsewhere. Many young, idealistic protestors loved their country but were pushing for reforms and improvements. The option of loving *and reforming or improving* was not stated in the false dilemma of "Love It or Leave It." Critical thinkers need to be aware of times when they are being urged to choose one of only two options. When this happens you need to ask yourself whether there any other possible options that you can select.

Appeal to authority is a form of fallacious reasoning that you are exposed to daily. Just turn on your television, and you will see many examples of this form of unsound reasoning. Authority figures are all too frequently used to persuade you to think a certain way or purchase a particular product. Famous athletes endorse soft drinks and breakfast cereals; the advertiser hopes you will think that if it is good enough for them, it's good enough for you. And what about the actor who plays a doctor on a prime-time program endorsing a brand of aspirin? Again, advertisers are playing on your beliefs that celebrity equals expertise or authority and that you will be persuaded to behave accordingly. Watch out! Evaluate claims for their factual information, not in terms of who is endorsing the product, the person, or the idea.

EVALUATING SOURCES OF INFORMATION

We are living in the "information age." There is an abundance of information available to us. You can find information in books, magazines, journals, and radio and television broadcasts and on the Internet. However, the mere fact that information is readily available does not mean it is credible and reliable. As a critical thinker, it is your responsibility to determine the veracity of the information by exercising careful judgment and evaluating the material according to certain criteria.

Information Literacy: Tools for Evaluation

Humboldt State University's library provides important guidelines to apply when evaluating any type of information from any source. The information that follows is taken (with minor modifications and additions) from their web site, **http://library.humboldt.edu.**

E X E R C I S E   6.3

EVALUATING CLAIMS

By reading newspapers and magazines or watching television, provide two examples of fallacious reasoning. The examples can come from news stories or product advertisements. Identify which of the types of fallacies your examples represent. Be specific and detailed.

1. _____

   _____

   _____

   _____

2. _____

   _____

   _____

   _____

Authority

Is the author an expert on the subject? What are the author's credentials? To find out, you can look at the source of the information to see what it tells you about the author. You can also see whether there have been any critical reviews of the author's work; these often provide information about the author and his or her expertise. Any information source that does not give the identity or credentials of the author/producer should be viewed as suspect and not deemed reliable. Beware: The Internet is notorious for this!

Timeliness

When was the information published? Is the date of publication important to understanding the subject under study? In some fields, such as medicine, science, business, and technology, it is important to use current information. For other fields, such as literature and history, older materials may be just as valuable as newer ones. Be sure to check with your instructor to find out on which time period your research should focus.

Documentation

Does the author refer to other publications/works? Does the source have a bibliography? Such data and reference material are critically important, for they indicate that the information is not merely the unsubstantiated opinions and claims of a single author. If the author has referred to the works of others, you should find a bibliography or list of references at the end of the source. *Hint:* Bibliographies often contain other excellent sources for your research.

Purpose

What is the purpose of the source? Is it to inform, persuade, present opinions, report research, or sell a product? For what audience is it intended (a popular audience or a scholarly audience)? Is the information biased? These are all very important questions that will help you assess the legitimacy of the information and determine whether it suits your research needs.

To determine the purpose of the source, read the information carefully and see whether it presents a balanced view of the topic (at least two sides of an issue should be addressed). In addition, examine whether an effort is being made to sell a product or promote a particular point of view. This is a strong indication of unbalanced information. Is the information published or authored by an organization with a particular interest or "agenda"? For example, say you read an article touting the health benefits of salt and then find that it is written by the president of the National Association of Sodium Producers. You can conclude that this author has a particular interest at stake and may not be unbiased in his or her reporting. Finally, is the information intended for a popular or a scholarly audience? In general, information written for popular or mass audiences is not highly technical and is not held to the same standards for publication as information written for scholarly audiences. A report on global warming published in *Newsweek* is not going to be as scientific as an article on the same topic published in a scientific scholarly journal. Ask your instructor whether popular or scholarly sources are expected for your assignment.

Review Process

Was the information reviewed before it was published or disseminated? The review process is important, because it helps to ensure the credibility and soundness of the information. In conducting a review, experts evaluate the particular book, article, film, performance, or broadcast. These experts judge the source according to certain criteria. If the experts agree that the information is sound, credible, and reliable, they usually recommend dissemination of the information. To find out whether a journal article is reviewed, check an issue of the journal. It will generally state that the publications are peer-reviewed or refereed. You can also consult *Ulrich's Periodicals Directory*, which lists journals and indicates if they are peer-reviewed. Additionally, you can consider the reputation of the publisher. Books and articles can be published by university presses, commercial publishers, associations, or government agencies. Knowing something about the publisher can help you assess the credibility of the source and identify bias and point of view. Ask your librarian for a reference source that will enable you to evaluate publishers. Four commonly used sources are *Literary Marketplace, Encyclopedia of Associations, AV Marketplace,* and *From Radical Left to Extreme Right.*

WARNING: Many Internet sites are not reviewed before being posted. Sites with the extension .edu (educational institutions) or .gov (government agencies) typically *do* go through some sort of review process and are generally viewed as credible.

Suitability

There are two key questions you need to ask yourself regarding this issue. Does the source contain the information you need? And is it written at a level you can understand? After perusing the information, determine whether the information is too general or too specific for your needs. When in doubt, consult your instructor.

Evaluating Web Sites

Just as you need to evaluate print information (books, magazines, journals) and broadcast information (television, radio), information found on the Web also needs to be scrutinized. An abundance of information exists on the Web. Much of it is good and reliable, but there is also a great deal of information that is biased, incorrect, and unreliable. The Reference Department at UCLA's Research Library has produced a guide to assist students in judging the quality of information on the Web. It has identified eight criteria that a good web site will meet. These guidelines are listed below, along with the steps that students must take to ascertain whether the site meets each standard. (Prepared by Patti Schifter Caravello, UCLA Charles E. Young Research Library Department. Reprinted with permission.)

1. Clearly states the author and/or organizational **source** of the information. *Students' task:*

   - Consider the qualifications, other works, and organizational affiliation of the author.
   - Look up the organization that produced the web site (if is not familiar) to identify its credentials, viewpoint, or agenda.
   - If the source is an e-journal, discover whether it is refereed (reviewed by scholars before it is accepted for publication).

Jeff Greenberg/Visuals Unlimited

2. Clearly states the **date** the material was written and the date the site was last revised. *Students' task:*

   • If the information is not current enough for your purposes or the date is not given, disregard the site.

3. Provides **accurate** data whose parameters are clearly defined. *Students' task:*

   • Compare the data found on the web site with data found in other sources (encyclopedias, reference books, articles, etc.) for accuracy, completeness, and recency.

   • Ask a librarian whether there are other important sources to check for this information.

4. Provides the **type** and **level** of information you need. *Students' task:*

   • Decide whether the level of detail and comprehensiveness, the treatment of the topic (scholarly or popular), and the graphics or other features are acceptable.

   • If the site does not provide the depth of coverage you need, look elsewhere.

5. Keeps **bias** to a minimum and clearly indicates point of view. *Students' task:*

   - Be aware that producing a web page does not require the checking and review that publishing a scholarly book requires; you may have retrieved nothing but someone's personal opinion on the topic.
   - Appealing graphics can distract you from even overt bias, so heighten your skepticism and examine the evidence (source, date, accuracy, level, and links).

6. Provides live **links** to related high-quality web sites. *Students' task:*

   - Click on several of the links provided to see whether they are active (an "error" message indicates that the links are not being maintained) and whether they are useful.
   - Check to see whether the criteria used to select the links are stated.

7. In the case of **commercial** sites, keeps the advertising sections separate from the content sections and does not let advertisers determine content. *Students' task:*

   - Look at the web address: .com means the site is produced by a company and may be commercial, include advertising, or offer to sell something.

8. Is clearly organized and designed for **ease of use**. *Students' task:*

   - Move around the page to see whether its organization makes sense and it is easy to return to the top or to the sections you need.
   - Decide whether the graphics enhance the content or detract from it.

COMPUTER   EXERCISE   6.4

EVALUATING INFORMATION SOURCES

For this exercise you will need a topic to research. Your instructor will assign you a research topic or give you the option of selecting your own. Make sure the topic is academic in nature (don't research the number of cylinders in the latest Honda Accord).

Using the Library to Find Sources

University libraries have a variety of online databases to locate sources.

1. List the major online databases that your university library has available. _____

_____

_____

_____

2. Using online databases, locate one newspaper or news magazine article and one journal article on your topic. Provide detailed information on how you located each source. For example, which databases did you use? How did you conduct the search (keywords used, author search, etc.)? _____

_____

_____

_____

Evaluating Sources

Evaluate the sources on the basis of the following criteria: authority, timeliness, documentation, purpose, review process, and suitability. Provide your instructor with a xerographic copy or printout of each of the information sources.

Evaluating Web Sites

1. Conduct an Internet search for information on your topic. Describe in detail how you conducted the search (search engines used, keywords, etc.).
2. Select two web sites that your search yielded and that provide information on your topic. Evaluate these sites using the eight guidelines listed in the "Evaluating Web Sites" section. Explain in detail how each site rates on these eight guidelines.

COMPUTER   APPLICATIONS

EVALUATING WEB SITES

Many of us use the Internet for research. However, not all web sites are equally credible. You must evaluate each web site to assess the quality and credibility of the information posted at that site. Here are four web sites that can help you do this.

Evaluating Web Sites: Criteria and Tools

    http://www.library.cornell.edu/okuref/research/webeval.html

Evaluating Quality on the Net

    http://www.tiac.net/users/hope/findqual.html

Thinking Critically About World Wide Web Resources

    http://www.library.ucla.edu/libraries/url/referenc/judging.html

Bibliography on Evaluating Internet Resources, by Nicole Auer

    http://refserver.lib.vt.edu/libinst/critTHINK.HTML

CHAPTER 7

Taking Exams

If you had kept track of all the exams you've taken in your academic life, it probably would make a nice big bonfire. Remember the spelling tests every Friday in elementary school, the weekly history tests in junior high, and your first essay exam? Clearly, you already have a long history of test taking. And most of you have been exposed to a wide variety of test types: multiple-choice, true/false, essay, and short-answer tests. Unfortunately, few (if any) teachers teach students **how** to prepare for exams and **how** to take them. There are numerous strategies and techniques that can help improve your performance on exams. Even though you have already spent some time in college, it is not too late to adopt these systems of test preparation and test taking. If you are a junior, you will still take at least 35–40 more exams and tests in your last two years of college. Furthermore, those of you who contemplate continuing your education after graduation will have to take standardized qualifying exams for acceptance into graduate and professional schools.

This chapter will provide you with techniques and strategies for test preparation and test taking. We will cover all the bases: identifying the different types of exams; how to organize your notes for the most efficient and effective studying; when, where, and how to study; and strategies to use when taking an exam. We will also address the very common problem of test anxiety and how to make that anxiety work for you, instead of against you.

DIFFERENT TYPES OF EXAMS

Professors use a variety of exam types to assess your progress and learning. Some instructors prefer one exam type, whereas many instructors use a variety of types of questions. It is important that you ask your instructor what type of exam she or he will be using. Different types of exams require different preparation strategies and test-taking techniques.

If your instructor tells you what type of exam will be given, you might want to ask whether he or she will provide examples of the types of questions that will be asked. Some instructors don't mind bringing sample questions to class.

The most common type of **objective exam** contains true/false and/or multiple-choice questions. Other varieties are fill-in-the-blank and matching tests. Objective exams mostly test you on factual material. These types of exams can be deceivingly difficult. You may think they are easy because information is contained in the question, and the answer itself is actually stated in multiple-choice and matching questions. However, well-crafted objective exams are often difficult and require ample preparation and familiarity with appropriate test-taking strategies.

Short-answer questions usually ask you to list, define, or describe something. The instructor is looking for a short and succinct answer. Brevity is desirable.

Essay questions test your command of factual information and your ability to analyze this information. An essay question will generally ask you to do one or more of the following things: analyze, define, illustrate, interpret, compare and contrast, criticize, describe, evaluate, discuss, or explain. To do any of these things, you must know the facts about the subject and provide evidence that you can think critically and independently about the topic. Strong essay answers usually take a position (have a thesis) and present factual, not emotional, information in support of that position.

Problem-solving questions are most often used in math and statistics courses, where you are given a problem and have to compute the answer. In your math and statistics courses, be sure to inquire whether you will be permitted to use a calculator or computer.

Standardized tests are rarely given in college courses. The SAT is an example of a standardized test. Entrance exams for graduate and professional schools are standardized. Most of theses exams contain objective questions but some also include essay items.

TEST PREPARATION: ORGANIZING YOUR NOTES

Basically, you need to find a method of studying that works for you. Organizing your notes is the first important step in this process. In most cases, you will have two sets of material that need to be organized so that you can use them to study effectively. One is your class lecture notes, and the other is your notes on your readings.

Organizing Lecture Notes

There are two basic methods that seem to work well in reviewing and organizing lecture notes. In order to use these systems effectively, you must have complete lecture notes. Ideally, you should read over your lecture notes shortly after you attend the lecture so that you can fill in any gaps in your notes while the material is still fresh in your mind. However, most students take their first

E X E R C I S E 7.1

DIFFERENT EXAM TYPES

1. List the number and types of exams you will have in each of your courses this term. If you don't have the information, now is a great time to contact your professors and ask them what they have planned.

   a. Course   _____

      Number of planned exams/quizzes   _____

      Types of exams/quizzes   _____

      _____

   b. Course   _____

      Number of planned exams/quizzes   _____

      Types of exams/quizzes   _____

      _____

   c. Course   _____

      Number of planned exams/quizzes   _____

      Types of exams/quizzes   _____

      _____

   d. Course   _____

      Number of planned exams/quizzes   _____

      Types of exams/quizzes   _____

      _____

   e. Course   _____

      Number of planned exams/quizzes   _____

      Types of exams/quizzes   _____

      _____

2. From your past test-taking experiences, which type of exam do you prefer? Which do you like least? Explain your preferences. Which type of exam do you generally perform well on? Is there any type on which you perform poorly? Why do you think your performance varies on different types of exams? (This is important; it is the beginning of a road map to help you overcome obstacles that you may have faced in the past.)

_____

_____

_____

_____

_____

_____

_____

_____

_____

3. Do you study differently when preparing for different types of exams? What are some of the differences in the way you study?

_____

_____

_____

_____

_____

_____

_____

_____

_____

_____

look at their notes shortly before it is time to take the exam. It is very important that you read over your notes *before* this time to see whether there are glaring gaps where the material does not make sense to you. If so, you will still have time to visit your instructor and ask questions on the confusing material.

One method for reviewing lecture notes is to read your notes from beginning to end for each lecture. In the left-hand margin of your notes, jot down major ideas, concepts, points, facts, etc. Do this for each page of your lecture notes. At the bottom of each page of notes, summarize in one or two sentences the information contained on that page. Using this method, you will have "notes on your notes." You will then study from these notes that you've taken on your lecture notes. We will refer to this note-taking system as the *within-notes method*.

Another method for reviewing lecture notes is the *flash card method*. Using 3×5- or 5×7-inch index cards write a term, formula, concept, fact, or event on one side of the card and its definition, explanation, or significance on the other side. Another use of flash cards is to go through your lecture notes and glean the most important information. Using one or more flash cards for each lecture, write an abbreviated outline of the lecture that contains only the major points and examples.

Organizing Textbook Notes

Highlighting important facts and concepts in your text is a useful and important step in the note-taking and review process. For the fortunate few with photographic memories, reading a passage once with highlights is sufficient to engrave the information forever into their brains, but the rest of us need to perform an additional step. We need to re-read the highlighted sections and take notes on the information. You can write notes in the margin of the text, or you can transfer the information to flash cards.

From discussing different strategies and methods of studying and test preparation, we know that what works for one student does not always work for another. Each of you has a preferred learning style. Some auditory learners obtain permission to tape their instructor's lectures and study by listening to the tapes. Visual learners do well by recopying their notes and using the flash card method. Rewriting the information on flash cards helps visual learners remember it. In short, find the method that works best for you and stick with it.

THE REVIEW PROCESS

Timing: When to Start Studying

In a perfect world, you would be reviewing your lecture notes each evening and keeping abreast of your reading assignments. Studying would be an ongoing and continuous process. Given the numerous demands on students, it is unrealistic to expect all students to keep current in all their courses. The following section on timing assumes that you have not been reviewing the course material throughout the term and are now faced with the unenviable task of compressing many weeks of material and review into several days (*not,* let's hope, a couple of hours!).

The first step is to review all of your lecture notes. Meet with your instructor to fill in any gaps or to get any necessary clarification on the material. The next step is to organize the notes you've taken on the lectures and assigned readings. Make sure you've taken "notes on your notes," using the flash card or within-notes method described above. About two days before the exam, start memorizing these flash card notes or the notes written in the margins of your lecture notes and texts. It is important to *refresh your memory a couple of hours before the exam.* Make this your final review. Reviewing up to the last nanosecond, as the instructor is passing out the exam, is counterproductive. You are not likley to gain any additional knowledge at this point, and such last-second cramming only serves to increase your anxiety.

E X E R C I S E 7.2

ORGANIZING YOUR NOTES

1. Take one week's worth of lecture notes from the course that is most difficult for you this term. Read over the notes. Are there gaps in your notes? If so, write down the questions that you will need to ask your instructor in order to fill in the gaps. Meet with or email your instructor to obtain the missing information.

2. Now that you have a complete set of lecture notes:

   a. Use the "within-notes" method of note taking, jotting down the major concepts, ideas, and facts in the margins of your lecture notes. In addition, at the bottom of each page of notes, write a summary, in one or two sentences, of the information on that page.

   b. For the same set of notes, use the flash card method. Write a concept, idea, term, formula, or fact on one side of each index card and the appropriate explanation or definition on the back. Or, you can write an abbreviated outline of your lecture notes on the flash cards.

   c. Which method do you prefer and why?

   d. Is there any other system or method that you use? What is it? What do you like about that technique? What are the disadvantages you have discovered of that particular technique?

Another situation to avoid is arriving at class too soon before the beginning of the exam. When you do, you inevitably hear students talk about what they studied and how they studied. If this differs from your experience, it can undermine your confidence. Nothing is to be gained by sitting in class with a bunch of apprehensive classmates. You're better off finding a quiet corner and meditating for a couple of minutes. Or stop by the cafeteria and have a healthful snack (save the sugar rush and chocolate reward for after the test).

Skimming and Cramming: A Last-Minute Strategy

We debated about whether we should include advice on how to engage in last-minute studying for an exam. Waiting until the night before an exam to begin reviewing the assigned readings and looking over lecture notes is a recipe for disaster. We can't imagine any college student deliberately putting himself or herself in such jeopardy. But we realize that some do sometimes find themselves in this precarious situation, so we decided to present techniques that may help you get acquainted with the material and may (we emphasize *may*) prevent you from failing the exam. No method, however, can make up for a lack of sus-

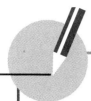

E X E R C I S E 7.3

EXAM PREPARATION DIARY

1. Obtain or draw a calendar for each month of this term. Make sure each week is represented. Number the weeks of the term on your calendar.

2. On your calendar, enter all of your exam and quiz dates, indicating the course, exam time, and date. Include the major topics the tests will cover.

3. This next step is important and is all too often omitted from planning calendars. Indicate on your calendar the times and days you plan to spend preparing for each test. State when you will start reviewing your lecture notes and assigned readings, when you will take notes on your notes (using the flash card or the "within-notes" method), and when you will do your final memorization of the information.

4. Describe ways in which this method of exam preparation is similar or dissimilar to the way you have prepared for exams in the past. What do you like, and what do you dislike, about this method?

tained or even sporadic attention to your course work. Waiting until the last minute to skim and cram is a very unwise strategy. Now that you've been warned. . . .

Skimming

Skimming is a quick way to get a sense of the contents of a chapter or article. This method of reading will not give you a deep understanding—only a superficial acquaintance with the material. Some readings are better suited for skimming than others. If your assigned reading contains an introduction and conclusion or summary, skimming is easier. Journal articles sometimes include, at the beginning of the article, an abstract (overall summary) of the article.

The first step in skimming is to read the introduction/abstract and conclusion. After reading these sections, you will have an idea of the topic of the reading, the major themes/theses, and the evidence or reasons presented in support of the main argument. Next, quickly read all headings, subheadings, graphs, and charts. Finally, read the first sentence of every paragraph. If you need to read more than the first sentence to gain a better understanding of the material, then do so. Also, pay special attention to words printed in bold type and words listed at the end of the chapter as key words and concepts. Know these. As you are skimming, take notes using one of the methods described earlier.

Cramming

This very problematic strategy requires that you focus on a small portion of all the material you will be tested on. Because you have not left yourself enough time to cover all the necessary material, you will need to determine, as best you can, what is the most important and essential information you will be tested on. Focus on that material and forget about the rest. It is better to know a lot about a small amount of material than to know nothing about all the material you should have covered. Concentrate on the essentials.

For the small amount of material on which you plan to focus, read over your lecture notes and the relevant assigned readings. Take notes on your lecture notes and readings. Whichever method of note taking you use, your task is to memorize the key concepts, terms, and facts. Recite the material aloud if you are an auditory learner. For visual learners, repeatedly writing the material will help you remember. The key to cramming is quick memorization of the essential material.

Study Groups: Pros and Cons

Getting together with classmates to prepare for an exam works well for some students and miserably for others. If you've never been involved in a study group, you might want to join one and evaluate whether this studying strategy is preferable, for you, to going solo.

Study groups offer several advantages:

- Shared information. All members of the study group will bring to these sessions their knowledge about the course material. There will be several sets of notes and different ideas and interpretations of the material. One student's weakness might be another student's strength. Group assistance and tutoring will naturally emerge.
- Emotional support. You're all experiencing the same stressful situation: preparing for an exam. Members can relate to each other's frustrations and anxieties, while still providing encouraging support. Be careful to build strengths and not encourage weaknesses.
- Mandatory study periods. By joining a study group, you are making a commitment to study. You are committed to attending set study sessions rather than procrastinating. You will probably study more often and for longer periods of time.

Study groups also have several disadvantages:

- Group conflict. Sometimes personality conflicts emerge in study groups. Precious time can be wasted on these personal antagonisms. Successful study groups usually have a person who assumes leadership responsibility and takes charge. This simply means that someone keeps the group on track and focused. The leader's responsibilities may include timing food breaks, limiting idle chat and gossiping, and maintaining group cohesion and civility.

There may be some group members who resent the leader, however, and conflicts will ensue, undermining the primary purpose of the group.

- Slackers. Not all members of a study group are equal in their level of knowledge and desire to contribute. Some members are moochers, contributing nothing and taking whatever they can. Someone who has missed most of the class meetings might join a study group in order to obtain other members' class notes, while contributing nothing to the group.

- Group composition. You may unwittingly join a group of students who are underperforming in class. Maybe they don't realize their comprehension of the material is insufficient, and the group may proceed under the false assumption that they are on the right track. Many hours and effort are then spent studying incorrect information. (Instructors sometimes can tell who has studied together when a group of students all miss the same exam questions.)

Mnemonics: Memory Aids

Mnemonics are techniques used to improve your memory, such as coming up with funny sayings or acronyms to help you remember complicated material. An example of a mnemonic used in elementary school to memorize the planets is "My mother used to serve everyone very nice juicy pickles." The first letter of each word (with the exception of the word *to*) represents the first letter of each of the nine planets: Mars, Mercury, Uranus, Saturn, Earth, Venus, Neptune, Jupiter, and Pluto. Medical students have used the mnemonic "HONC if you like life!" to remember the four elements that make up life's building blocks: hydrogen, oxygen, nitrogen, and carbon. And to remember the three body organs that are the sites of 50% of all the cancers, they use "College lunch is best" to evoke the colon, lungs, and breasts.

The key to a successful mnemonic is to create a positive, funny, or peculiar image or sentence. Rude or sexual rhymes seem to be the easiest to remember (so use them, just keep them private!). Whatever mnemonic you create, it needs to be powerful enough to be easily remembered and immediately linked to the information it is intended to evoke.

TAKING THE EXAM

We will discuss strategies for taking three types of exams: objective exams, essay exams, and standardized tests.

Objective Exams

Students generally love true/false and multiple-choice questions. Maybe they've figured out that with true/false questions they have a 50% chance of *guessing* the correct answer. With multiple-choice questions, they have a 25% chance of guessing the correct answer (assuming that there are four answers to choose

EXERCISE 7.4

MNEMONICS

1. For each of the following items, create a mnemonic. Although we have admitted that the best mnemonics are often rude, crude, and sexual, please refrain from using obscene material for this exercise. (We need to protect your instructors!)

   a. The first ten amendments to the U.S. Constitution. (You'll have to look these up.) *Hint:* Look in the back of a U.S. government textbook or surf the Web.

   Mnemonic _____

   _____

   _____

   b. The ten systems of the human body (respiratory, muscular, reproductive, urinary, nervous, endocrine, circulatory, digestive, skeletal, skin). Use any order you wish.

   Mnemonic _____

   _____

   _____

2. Select something from your course work and create a mnemonic for it.

   Item _____

   _____

   _____

   Mnemonic _____

   _____

   _____

from). However, well-designed objective questions can present a challenge, even when you know the material. First, be sure to read the questions very carefully. Look for absolute terms such as *always, all, never,* and *must.* If a sentence contains an absolute term, chances are it is false. Very few things in life are absolute. Qualifying terms such as *often, perhaps, many,* and *sometimes* indicate that the statement is probably true.

Union members always vote Democratic.

Union members often vote Democratic.

The first statement is false, because union members don't always, without exception, vote Democratic. The second statement is true, because union members overall do vote Democratic.

Another important point about true/false questions is that the entire statement must be true for the answer to be true. If part of a statement is false and part is true, you must declare the answer to be false.

The solar system has nine planets, with Pluto being closest to Earth.

It is true that our solar system has nine planets, but Pluto is not the planet closest to Earth. Therefore, the statement must be marked false.

Also, watch out for tricky or confusing questions. The use of double negatives in a question is confusing. You should reword such a question and then determine whether it is true or false. These questions are usually quite difficult to unravel, as you can see from this statement:

Not viewing televised political ads does not have an impact on voting turnout rates.

What a question! Help! Possible translation: "Those who don't view televised political ads vote at the same rate as those who do view the ads."

Noticing patterns of answers can sometimes be helpful. For example, a long string of true answers will probably be broken by a false answer, and vice versa. Likewise, with multiple-choice questions, look for patterns in the sequence of answers. The first listed answer is less likely than the others to be the correct answer. And remember, as you are reviewing the choices, that you need to select the *best answer presented,* which is not always the perfect answer. Sometimes, instructors unintentionally give away an answer to a question by stating the answer in another question. Here's an example: a government exam includes the true/false item "There are 11 amendments in the Bill of Rights." Later on in the exam, this multiple-choice question appears:

The Bill of Rights, containing the first 10 amendments to the U.S. Constitution, generally protects: a. citizens from noncitizens; b. citizens from the government; c. citizens from foreign nations; d. all of the above.

As you can see, the earlier true/false question has been answered in another exam question. Be on the lookout for these "gifts." This is a good reason to review the test and your answers, if time remains, rather than turning in the test early.

As you take the test, first answer the questions you are sure of. Circle the number of the questions you don't know the answers to. If you waste valuable time pondering the questions you don't know the answers to, you may not have enough time to answer the questions you can answer correctly. If time permits, go back to those unanswered questions and use some of the strategies outlined above. If there are no penalties for wrong answers, then guess. Do not leave any questions unanswered if you will not be penalized. You have a 25%–50% chance of guessing correctly, but you have a 0% chance if you leave it blank.

One last word of advice on taking objective tests. Don't change your answers unless you are positive you are changing your answer from an incorrect one to a correct one. Research has shown that your first answer is more likely to be the correct one. Also, read the questions carefully, but don't read too much into them. Interpret them at face value; don't overanalyze the question, reading things into it that the instructor had not intended.

Essay Exams

Many of you have had limited experience in taking essay exams. There are some general guidelines that you should follow when writing an answer to an essay exam. First, read the question very carefully. It is not uncommon for an essay question to contain a few questions within the larger question. For example, the question might ask you first to describe an event, then to compare it with other events, and finally to explain or evaluate some aspects of the event. This question has three parts: It asks you first to describe, second to compare, and finally to evaluate. You need to answer the parts in that precise order. Thus, on your initial reading of the essay question, determine whether there are questions within the question, and start separating out the individual questions to be addressed.

The next step is to jot down (on a separate scrap paper or in the margin of your exam sheet) all the information you know about the topic. Ideally, you should start to outline your answer. Your essay answer should contain as much detailed information as possible. This is where a command of the facts has enormous payoffs. State the important and relevant names, dates, events, and ideas. With essay questions, the more concrete information you provide, the better.

In an essay question, you may be asked to take a position and support it. In these instances, you state your position (thesis) clearly and provide evidence in support of your position. Do not argue from emotions, feelings, likes, or preferences, unless specifically asked to do so. Use factual information to support your thesis.

Some advice: If you don't know the answer and don't have any knowledge on the topic, do not attempt to answer the question. Nothing annoys an in-

E X E R C I S E 7.5

MOCK EXAMS

Your instructor will provide you with practice exams representing both objective and essay exams. Follow your instructor's directions. Your instructor will review the exams in class, indicating exam strategies that are appropriate to use.

structor more than reading a lot of nonsense that is totally unrelated to the topic. It wastes the instructor's time and puts him or her in a bad mood in grading the rest of your exam.

Standardized Tests

If you are planning to pursue a graduate degree, most universities require that you take a standardized admissions test. Your score on the admissions test will probably be the most important factor in determining whether you are accepted into your chosen postgraduate program and school(s). Professional schools generally require the GMAT for medical school, the LSAT for law school, and the GRE for a variety of graduate programs. These tests are standardized in that all those who take them are given nearly identical tests. These exams measure your abilities and knowledge in several areas: verbal, quantitative, analytical, and subject area.

Libraries and bookstores have review guides for all of the major standardized tests. Many of these guides contain sample and practice questions. Private companies often provide courses in test preparation for specific standardized exams. These preparation courses are costly. However, the larger, better-known companies often offer reduced rates or scholarships for those students in need of financial assistance.

One important strategy for doing well on these exams is to prepare and study well in advance of the exam. You cannot cram for these tests. Allow yourself at least a few months to prepare by reading the review book and practicing with the sample questions and exams. Do not officially register for and take an exam unless you are prepared. All results become part of your official record. Do not "practice" by taking the official exam. Use the practice questions in the review book for this purpose.

EXAM ANXIETY

Very few students enjoy taking exams. A number of students experience anxiety before and sometimes during an exam. It is common for students who are anxious about an upcoming exam to procrastinate and engage in various avoidance techniques. Watching excessive amounts of TV, sleeping during the day, organizing and cleaning their surroundings, overeating, and other behaviors that take your mind off studying are all examples of avoidance behaviors. Fear and anxiety paralyze students in this pre-exam stage. Time is not budgeted properly, so in the end, not enough time is allocated to review notes, fill in the gaps, meet with instructors, and perhaps join a study group.

One of the most successful strategies to reduce pre-exam anxiety and to avoid anxiety during the exam is to be prepared. The familiarity you have with the material will ease your mind, give you confidence, and reduce anxiety. How, then, do you get over the hurdle of procrastination, especially for a course that is troublesome? Set up a schedule and force yourself to review your lecture notes and readings for just 15 minutes a day, starting two weeks before the exam date. Slowly increase the time you spend studying, allocating longer periods of time in the days immediately prior to the test. It is critical that you take this first small step to break the avoidance pattern, and an added benefit is that you acquaint yourself with the material.

Stress-Reducing Techniques

Here are some helpful exercises to help you relax if you feel yourself "clutching" and losing focus during an exam.

- If permitted, select a seat where you feel most comfortable. Arrive early enough to have your choice of seats, but not so early that you are exposed to all the pre-exam nervous chatter.
- Practice controlled breathing. Take deep breaths and exhale slowly. When we're nervous, we tend to hold our breath. Deep and deliberate inhaling and slow exhaling will help reduce your anxiety level.
- Visualization is known to reduce stress. Visualize a pleasant and calming scene. Maybe it soothes you to picture yourself swimming in a lake, skiing down a slope, or napping in a hammock. Whatever soothes you, use it.
- Don't watch other students. There will inevitably be students who finish the exam in record time. Most students get nervous when a classmate turns in the exam in half the time allocated. Rest assured, the overwhelming majority of those who finish in record time perform poorly. Their answers are incorrect or insufficient, and that's why they finished so quickly. Don't pay any attention to them.
- Positive thinking works. Tell yourself that you can and will perform well. Before the exam, picture yourself taking it with ease. Repeat this visualization. On the day of the exam, steer clear of nervous, negative students. Instead, spend the time pumping yourself up psychologically.
- Answer the questions you know first. Don't get stumped or stymied by the difficult ones. Just pass over them and come back to answer them if time permits.

If you know you have a serious problem with test anxiety, then see a professional. Visit your campus health center, where counselors specialize in this sort of problem. In fact, many colleges and universities have workshops and support groups dealing specifically with this issue.

APPROPRIATE EXAM BEHAVIOR

1. Arrive on time for the exam. Walking in late communicates to the instructor that you don't take the exam seriously. Often the instructor announces important information about the exam at the beginning of the exam period. Many instructors don't feel compelled to inform the tardy student of these earlier, important announcements. And, of course, from a purely practical standpoint, arriving late reduces the time available to take the exam. Don't count on the instructor allowing you to stay longer to make up the difference.

2. Bring the essentials: Blue book and/or Scantron (available in university bookstore), pens/pencils, dictionary (if permitted), calculator (if needed and permitted), and any other materials your instructor has requested. Inquire whether you have permission to bring food and drinks into the exam. Do not bring headphones.

3. Keep your answer sheet or exam covered. There are apt to be roving eyes, and you don't want to be accused of complicity in cheating.

4. Bathroom visit. Before entering the classroom to take your exam, be sure to visit the restroom. Many instructors do not permit students to leave the room while the exam is in progress. (There have been cases of notes being stashed in the restroom to be reviewed during a bathroom break.)

5. Leave all electronic equipment (cell phones, pagers, etc.) at home or in your car. If you must have your phone or pager with you, turn off the ringer.

E X E R C I S E 7.6

EXAM ANXIETY

1. Do you suffer from pre-exam anxiety? Describe your symptoms. What do you believe causes these feelings? How could you alleviate this problem?

_____

_____

_____

_____

_____

_____

_____

_____

_____

_____

2. Do you experience anxiety during an exam? What usually happens? How do you generally cope with the situation? How could you prevent the occurrence of exam anxiety or minimize it? How could you improve your coping mechanisms when it does occur?

_____

_____

_____

_____

_____

_____

_____

_____

_____

_____

Gary Conner/PhotoEdit

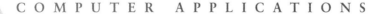

COMPUTER APPLICATIONS

EXAM AND TEST-TAKING WEB SITES

A web site owned by Princeton Review, which produces most of the standardized college and graduate school admissions tests, can be accessed at **http://www.Review.com**. This site posts full-length samples of the GRE, MCAT, and other exams.

For helpful hints on test taking, visit **http://www.iss.stthomas.edu/studyguides/ tsttak.html**. This site offers tips on taking objective and essay exams.

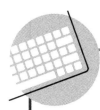

C O M P U T E R   E X E R C I S E   7.7

EXAM-TAKING STRATEGIES

1. Many college and university web sites provide helpful hints on test taking. They cover topics such as how to study effectively, how to deal with exam anxiety, and strategies for taking different types of exams. Using an Internet search engine (see the Computer Applications box on web search engines in Chapter 8 for some suggestions), locate test-taking web sites. (*Hint:* Type in the keywords "test taking" in the search box.) Visit the sites found in your search, and review the information provided.

2. List the seven strategies and recommendations that you believe are the most helpful. Indicate where you found this information (cite the web site address). For each of the items you list, briefly explain why this is an important strategy for you to adopt and why you believe it will improve your test performance.

_____

_____

_____

_____

_____

_____

_____

_____

_____

_____

_____

_____

_____

_____

_____

_____

The Library Research Paper

The second most dreaded statement a student can hear is "This course requires a library research paper." (The *most* dreaded is "Take out a blank sheet of paper and put your name on it.") Yes, the dreaded term paper! Most of you have never been shown how to research and write a comprehensive paper. In fact, we know of numerous students who shop for professors who do not assign term papers, hoping to graduate without ever having to endure this torture. But in many cases, it is unavoidable. You must take a certain course to graduate, and that course requires a research paper.

Professors usually assign the paper early in the term and expect students to work throughout the term on the paper. Pulling an all-nighter won't work here. You cannot conduct research and write a satisfactory paper in a couple of days. Furthermore, most professors leave you on your own. They don't check up on you throughout the term to monitor your progress. They trust that you are working on your paper and that if you need assistance, you will contact them.

Research papers differ from other types of papers in some important ways. Obviously, research papers require that you engage in research. In addition to information on your topic, many instructors expect to see evidence of higher-order thinking skills in the paper you turn in. It is assumed that you will carefully evaluate and think about the information you have collected and present cogent arguments and analyses.

Most of you have probably had papers assigned that did not require any library or outside research. You lucked out! Perhaps your instructor asked you to write a paper about your opinion on a contemporary issue without requiring you to research the topic. This type of paper is sometimes referred to as a "thought piece." Or maybe you were assigned a type of biographical paper describing your life or the experiences of a family member, or perhaps a paper analyzing a poem or short story. Research papers are more comprehensive than these types of papers and require very careful planning and execution. In this section, we provide an in-depth discussion about writing the library research paper and offer some tips and guidelines to assist you in this activity.

THE RESEARCH PROCESS

In *The Short Handbook for Writers*, Schiffhorst and Pharr divide the research process into the following four steps:

Step 1.

Beginning the research

Choosing an interesting subject

Selecting a limited topic

Developing a working thesis

Step 2.

Locating and skimming sources

Searching for information relevant to your working thesis

Eliminating irrelevant information

Reexamining your working thesis

Step 3.

Reading sources and drawing conclusions

Reading selected sources carefully

Taking detailed notes

Analyzing the information

Developing a thesis statement

Step 4.

Writing the paper

Composing the first draft

Revising the paper

Adding documentation

Formatting and editing the final draft

Preparing the Works Cited or References page

Proofreading and submitting the paper

Now let's review these steps, one by one. You will see that breaking down the paper-writing process into more manageable steps makes it easier to deal with. As you complete each step, you can be confident that you are researching and writing a sophisticated college level research paper.

Step 1: Beginning the Research

Before you can begin your research, you need to determine the topic of your paper. For some of your courses, the instructor will assign you a topic; at other times, you will have the freedom to select a topic on your own. Topics can be very specific (the migration patterns of the purple polka-dotted sparrows in the subtropical rainforests), or you could be asked to write a paper on a broader topic (U.S. foreign policy in the 20th century). In some instances, an instructor will give you a general topic and expect you to narrow its focus for your paper.

Selecting a Topic

When you are required to select a topic, there are some basic guidelines you should consider. First, pick a topic that interests you. This will make the research and writing less arduous and more enjoyable. The one cautionary note here is to stay away from highly emotional, controversial topics such as abortion, prayer in schools, capital punishment, and other "hot button" issues. The main problem with these topics is that it can be very difficult to remain objective during the research and writing stages. It is too easy to fall into emotional, subjective, polemical argumentation that is not indicative of higher-order, rational analysis.

Another consideration in the selection of your topic is the quantity of research available on the issue you are examining. Some fascinating topics might prove very difficult to research because there is little information available. A more common problem is selecting a topic where there is an overabundance of information. It then becomes difficult to weed through the material to grasp the basic issues and arguments related to that topic.

Narrowing the Focus

Topics that are very large in scope (such as "religion and government") cannot be dealt with adequately in a term paper. Does this mean you cannot select interesting, relevant topics in these areas? Of course not. What you would need to do is narrow the focus of the topic to a more specific issue. If you were interested in the interplay between religion and government, you would need to come up with a specific topic related to the more general one. For example, you might want to narrow the topic to the use of government-supported vouchers for private religious schools, or to Blue Laws (local ordinances prohibiting certain activities on Sunday) in selected communities, or to the incorporation of Judeo-Christian values into governmental ethics laws. This narrowing of the topic provides you with the necessary direction for your library research and writing.

What if you don't know enough about the general topic to start narrowing the focus? There is a simple solution. The first step is to start researching the broad topic. You can look up the topic in an encyclopedia and read an overview or summary of the important aspects and issues related to it. Reading the

EXERCISE 8.1

STEP 1: BEGINNING THE RESEARCH

If you have a topic that needs to be researched for a course assignment, use that topic in this exercise. If you do not have such an assignment, select a topic being covered in one of your courses.

1. Topic of research: _____

2. Narrowing the topic

   a. The general topic is _____.

   b. I have narrowed the general topic to the more specific topic of _____.

   c. Describe the steps you took in narrowing the topic. What library resources did you use? How did they help you narrow the topic? For example, did you consult the *Reader's Guide*? Did you use an online database search? How did you locate news articles on your topic? How many articles did you read to gain background information? List the articles you read. In general, what was the method you employed to narrow the focus of your topic?

   _____

   _____

   _____

   _____

   _____

   d. What is your working thesis?

   _____

   _____

   e. How did you arrive at this thesis?

   _____

   _____

encyclopedia will help you generate some ideas about narrowing the topic. Another recommendation is to go to a library and find *The Reader's Guide to Periodical Literature*. If you look in the subject index, it will provide you with subtopics on your general topic and will indicate how many articles have been published in magazines and periodicals for each of these subtopics. This will generate ideas on how to narrow your topic and also give you a sense of how much material is available. Third, you can do a computerized online search of your library's databases. This is probably the quickest and most comprehensive way to search for information.

Developing a Thesis Statement

After you decide on your topic, your next step is to develop a working thesis statement. A thesis is the central idea, or main point, of your paper. Writing a paper using higher-order thinking skills requires that you take a position on a main point in your paper

When first researching your paper, you will be guided by what is called a working thesis. This is the general point of your paper, but the more research you conduct on your topic, the more explicit and refined your thesis will become. For example, if your topic is global warming and urban transportation, your working thesis could be "Global warming will continue unless more environmentally friendly automobiles are manufactured." This working thesis will guide your research activities. You will look for sources that address this issue. After gathering and reading information on this topic, you will probably have a more specific central point that you want to argue in your paper. (This will be discussed in Step 3.)

Step 2: Locating and Skimming Sources

When searching for information relevant to the working thesis, you will need to go to your campus library. You have probably had a tour of the library. If you haven't, inquire about how you can sign up for a visit. Once in the library, you will need to determine what types of sources you need. Follow your professor's instructions. You may have been told to use newsmagazines, or scholarly journals, or original documents, or other sources of information. Inform the librarian of your particular information needs.

Some universities have numerous libraries, each focusing on specific disciplines. There may be a medical library, law library, social sciences library, and/or humanities library. Other campuses have one large all-encompassing library. Get acquainted with your particular library and its resources and—more important—find a friendly librarian to ask for advice and direction on seeking out the sources you need for your research. If you have a class handout explaining your paper assignment, *bring it with you and show it to the librarian.* This will clarify for the librarian exactly what information sources are needed. You will probably use computerized library databases to search for your sources. The librarian will assist you in this process.

COMPUTER APPLICATIONS

WEB SEARCH ENGINES

Search engines help people locate information on the Web. There are numerous search engines available. Basically, a search engine has millions of web pages indexed by key-words. When you type in your keyword(s), the search engine reviews these millions of web pages, locating those documents that contain the keywords you selected. Here are some of the better-known search engines and their web sites:

Alta Vista	**www.altavista.com**
Lycos	**www.lycos.com**
Google	**www.google.com**
Excite	**www.excite.com**
Yahoo	**www.yahoo.com**
Infoseek	**www.infoseek.com**
HotBot	**www.hotbot.com**

Try more than one search engine when researching your keyword(s). The various search engines use different methods of locating documents. You will be surprised to discover that the different engines often retrieve different sources of information on your topic.

Primary and Secondary Sources

Sources fall into two general categories: primary and secondary. In researching your topic, you may have occasion to use both primary and secondary sources. Sometimes your instructor will indicate a preference for primary over second-ary sources, or vice versa. What's the difference? **Primary sources** can be thought of as original sources of information. An example is the *Declaration of Independence*. When you read the original document (or a copy of it), you are using a primary source. When you read someone's essay interpreting the *Declaration of Independence,* on the other hand, you are using a **secondary source.** Scientific data, artwork, plays, literature, survey results, historical doc-uments, government reports, and news reports are all primary sources. Inter-pretations, critiques, analyses, commentaries, and reviews are secondary sources. Typically, if your instructor doesn't mention whether you are to use primary or secondary sources, you can feel free to use either or both. When in doubt, check with your instructor.

Seth Resnick/Stock Boston

Relevant and Irrelevant Information

When reviewing sources, remember to evaluate them in terms of the criteria stated in Chapter 6. If you are confident that the source is reliable and credible, then you must determine whether the information is relevant to your topic and working thesis. If the source addresses your research topic and provides support for your working thesis, consider it relevant information and take notes on it. What if the source provides support for a *counterargument* to your thesis? Information supporting a position contrary to yours is not just relevant but crucial. Sophisticated thinkers always acknowledge the arguments in opposition to their own thesis and indicate how those arguments are weak and/or flawed. Thus these sources are also important, and you should definitely include them in your detailed notes. At this stage, it is also important to eliminate irrelevant information, even though it might be interesting. If it doesn't address your central theme, discard it.

Working Outlines

This initial reading of numerous sources will provide you with enough information to formulate a working outline for your paper. You already have your working thesis (your central point). Now you are ready to identify the points that will support your thesis. Arrange these points in a logical order—and *voilà*, you have a rough outline. Then reevaluate your original working thesis to see whether it is still valid. The sources you've skimmed may have provided you with information that necessitates a modification of your original working thesis.

Let's suppose our original working thesis has not changed: "Global warming will continue unless more environmentally friendly automobiles are manufactured." We now list our major points in support of this thesis. We list them as the first-level topics in an outline:

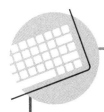

C O M P U T E R   E X E R C I S E   8.2

STEP 2: LOCATING AND SKIMMING SOURCES

For this exercise you will continue using the topic you selected in Exercise 8.1 (Step 1: Beginning the Research).

1. Go to the campus library and locate four articles on your topic. One of the articles must come from a scholarly journal (some databases call these "refereed" or "reviewed" articles). The remaining three may come from newspapers and/or magazines. Use your library's online databases to locate your four references. If your library has more than one online database, use at least two different databases to locate your articles. List the databases you used. List the keyword(s) you used. Indicate which keyword(s) resulted in the most successful searches. Remember, "most successful" doesn't mean the search that results in the greatest number of finds but, rather, the search that yields the articles that are most useful for your paper.

2. For each of the four articles, provide the name(s) of the author(s), date of publication, name of publication, title of article, volume number, and issue number (if available). *Note:* Online searches produce either the full text of an article or an abstract, which is a very brief summary of the article. If you are provided only with an abstract, you will need to locate the article in the library and read the full text.

3. Skim each of these sources and (a) note how you evaluated the credibility of each source, employing the criteria from the section "Evaluating Sources of Information" in Chapter 6; (b) briefly explain how each meets your research needs; and (c) indicate whether the sources are primary or secondary.

4. Develop a rough outline for your paper.

I. Scientific evidence suggests that Earth's temperature has been increasing because of pollutants.
II. Automobile emissions are a primary factor in pollution.
III. The automobile industry has been manufacturing higher-polluting vehicles, especially SUVs.
IV. Experimental vehicles (mostly electronic cars) reduce harmful emissions associated with global warming.

Step 3: Reading Sources and Drawing Conclusions

Now that you've located the sources you need for your paper, it is time to take detailed notes. Everyone eventually finds a note-taking system that suits his or her needs (see the section "Note Taking from Written Material" in Chapter 5). Here are some suggestions, which you can modify.

Note-Taking Strategies

First, you will need some note cards. We recommend 4×6-inch note cards. Each source will have its own note card, on which you will record the following information:

1. Author's name, title of source, date of publication, volume number, and issue number (if available).
2. Library location (call number) or Internet URL address.
3. Keywords identifying the subject or theme of the source.
4. Page number(s).
5. Notation indicating whether your note card contains a summary of the information, a direct quote, or a paraphrase.

For each of the sources, you will need to decide whether you want to write a brief summary of the source, whether you want to use a direct quote from the source, and whether you want to paraphrase a few ideas from the source.

1. *Summarizing the source.* If you don't plan to use any direct quotes or paraphrasing, then it makes sense just to summarize the material. A summary briefly records the most important facts contained in the source.

2. *Direct quotes.* In *Easywriter* (New York: St. Martin's Press, 1997), Lunsford and Connors point out, "Quote—use an author's exact words—when the wording expresses a point so well that you cannot change it without weakening it; when the author is a respected authority whose opinion supports your own ideas; or when an author disagrees profoundly with others in the field" (1997: 128). On your note card, copy the quotation exactly as it appears in the source, and place quotation marks around the direct quote (as I placed quotation marks around the words of Lunsford and Connors). You will need to consult a writing style manual for more specific information on how to incorporate quotations into the text of your paper.

EXERCISE 8.3

STEP 3: READING SOURCES AND DRAWING CONCLUSIONS

1. Take notes on the four sources you've located, using the guidelines presented in this section. Use summarizing, direct quotes, and paraphrasing techniques. See Chapter 5 for more information on note-taking techniques. Turn your note cards in to your instructor.

2. Refine your working thesis. Explain how you developed the final thesis or central point for your paper.

_____

_____

_____

_____

_____

_____

_____

_____

_____

_____

3. Select an organizational/analytical style for your paper. Explain why you selected that style.

_____

_____

_____

_____

_____

_____

_____

_____

_____

_____

_____

3. *Paraphrasing.* To paraphrase is to put the author's major ideas into your own words. However, if you use three or more consecutive words of the author, then you must use quotation marks and treat it as a direct quote. When you paraphrase, or reword someone else's ideas, you still must give credit to the author, so don't forget to write the author's name and year of publication on your note card.

After you have completed this step, it is time to analyze the information on which you've taken notes.

Analyzing the Information

There are different ways to analyze and organize information for a research paper. Your instructor will often dictate the analytical scheme you are to use. Perhaps your professor wants you to select a topic that reflects a problem and to analyze various solutions (urban pollution and automobiles). Or maybe you'll be asked to write a "compare and contrast" research paper (functions of the mass media in democratic and in totalitarian political regimes). See the section "Organizational and Analytical Styles of Papers" in this chapter.

Developing the Final Thesis Statement

After you have conducted your library research and reflected on and analyzed the information, you will need to revise your working thesis to reflect a more pointed, central idea. The working thesis stated earlier, "Global warming will continue unless more environmentally friendly automobiles are manufactured," could be revised to "Metropolitan areas with populations over one million need to have stringent automobile emissions standards in order to minimize local pollution and improve air quality." This final version of your thesis will appear in your paper as the central, guiding point.

Step 4: Writing the Paper

The topic we've selected, pollution and automobiles, is an example of a "problem–solution" paper. But regardless of the analytical or organizational style, the steps involved in writing the paper are essentially the same.

Writing the First Draft

The first, critically important step is to compose the first draft, also referred to as a rough draft, of your paper. In writing your first draft, you will use all of the information you have gathered. Rough drafts generally are written quickly and are somewhat disorganized. The purpose of a first draft is to get your ideas and arguments on paper. You will have ample opportunity to fine-tune your paper during the revision stage. Unfortunately, many students write their papers the night before they are due, not giving themselves time to re-read and rewrite weak sections of the paper.

Revising Your Paper

Read your draft to see whether you need to revise or change any of the concepts contained in your paper, the presentation of information and argumentation, the organization of the paper, the use of quotations and paraphrasing, and/or the focus and scope of your paper.

Adding More Documentation

At this point, you may notice the need to add more documentation to bolster or modify some of your points or arguments. This may require doing additional library research or simply incorporating more of the information you had gathered earlier but had not used.

Editing and Proofing Your Final Draft

It might take two, three, or even four more drafts before you are satisfied with your paper and have the final draft. Before turning in the final draft of your paper, you need to perform another critical step in the revising process: formatting and editing the final draft. Students often overlook this step, but most instructors will penalize you for handing in a paper that is sloppily organized or contains misspelled words and typos. This indicates to the instructor that you did not spend much time reviewing and rewriting your paper. Editing the final draft consists of checking carefully for spelling errors (by all means, use the Spell Check function of your word processing software), eliminating any grammatical errors, and using proper punctuation and sentence structure. You also need to be sure you are using the correct margin settings. Remember to use the documentation/citation style requested by your instructor. And always turn in a typed paper. (Unless the instructor specifically states that a handwritten paper is acceptable, the assumption is that all work is to be typed.)

ORGANIZATIONAL AND ANALYTICAL STYLES OF PAPERS

There are four general styles that can be used to present information in a research paper. Sometimes a combination of styles is appropriate for a given topic. The Research and Education Association's *Writing an A+ Research Paper* describes the four basic analytical styles.

1. *Chronological.* Describe the topic in a chronological manner—that is, according to when the important events took place. *Example:* If your paper topic were U.S. foreign policy toward China, you would provide information on U.S. relations with China from the earliest times to the present day, explaining when, how, and why major changes in policy came about.

2. *Compare and contrast.* Describe how the elements of your topic are similar and how they are different. *Example:* If your paper topic were the mating habits of marine mammals, you would discuss areas in which the behaviors of dolphins and whales are similar and the ways in which they differ. You would offer scientific explanations for the similarities and differences.

3. *Topical.* Break a very general topic down into more specific fragments and analyze each fragment. *Example:* If your topic were television's influence on campaign politics, you could discuss the influence of televised political ads, the effect of televised debates on the electorate, and the impact of news stories about the candidates.

4. *Problem–solution.* Select a problem and either analyze the efficacy of various solutions or come up with your own solution, which is supported by the research. *Example:* Addressing the topic of urban pollution and automobile emissions, you would review the research on automobile emissions contributing to pollution in urban areas and discuss solutions offered by various groups such as the auto industry and environmental organizations, pointing out which solutions are believed to be effective and why, and which are perceived to be ineffective and why.

THE FIVE-PART RESEARCH PAPER

There are five main parts to a library research paper. Your instructor may want you to write your paper in a different format, so be sure to check with your instructor to find out his or her preferences. If your instructor does not provide you with any specific guidelines, the following organizational format should be used.

I. **Introduction.** The introduction contains a brief statement introducing your paper topic. The next step is to state why your topic is important for study. And finally, you will indicate the purpose of your paper. Is your purpose to explain, describe, or persuade? The introduction is where you state your thesis if the purpose of your paper is persuasion/argumentation. The introduction need not be any longer than 1–1½ pages.

II. **Review of the Literature.** In this section you will very briefly summarize the information you collected during your library research. Remember to use the citation style (MLA, APA, Chicago) preferred by your instructor. Summarize the main point(s) of every reference you refer to in your paper. A varied writing style works best, mixing paraphrasing with direct quotes. Be brief. As a rule of thumb, don't devote more than a quarter of a page to each reference. Group those references together that address the same issue. Example: "Smith (1998), Doe (1990), and Jones (1989) all found automobile emissions to have increased anywhere from six- to tenfold in urban areas during the 1980s. In contrast, Ford (1999) and Olds and Chevy (1990) found a 2% reduction in auto emissions from 1975 to 1985."

III. **Discussion.** This section begins by restating the topic and purpose of your paper. If you have a thesis, restate it here. It is in this section that you will use one of the four analytical/organizational styles discussed in the previous section. If you were using the problem–solution format, you would begin by describing the problem, then discussing the various solutions that have been proposed, and ending with your evaluation of the strengths and weaknesses of each solution. If you have a position you are advocating (thesis), the discussion section is where you will provide the research and evidence to support your thesis. The length of this section varies, and you should check with your instructor.

IV. **Conclusion.** This is a very short section in which you restate the purpose of your paper, summarize the major points/arguments/findings, and make a final statement.

V. **References.** This section will contain a list of all the materials you referred to in your paper. Be sure to consult with your instructor to determine which citation style to use.

Your instructor may want your paper to include additional sections, such as an Appendix, Abstract, etc.

CITATION STYLES

Whenever you use information from any source, you need to reference or cite that source. There are three major citation formats: MLA (from the Modern Languages Association), APA (from the American Psychological Association), and the "Chicago" style (from *A Manual of Style,* published by the University of Chicago Press). The MLA format is used primarily for research papers in the fields of English, the humanities, and foreign languages. The APA citation style is used for papers in the social sciences, education, and technical writing. Both the MLA and APA styles use what is called parenthetical citations, rather than footnotes or endnotes. With parenthetical citations, the name of the author(s), the year of publication, and the page number for direct quotes are inserted in parentheses in the text (body) of your paper. With the Chicago style, this information is contained in a footnote placed at the bottom of the page.

EXERCISE 8.4

STEP 4: WRITING THE PAPER

1. Using the organizational/analytical style you selected in Exercise 8.3, write a first draft of your paper. Your paper should consist of five parts: Introduction, Review of the Literature, Discussion, Conclusion, and Bibliography. Because you are using only four sources for this paper, the length of the paper will be only about 3–4 pages plus the bibliography. If your instructor does not specify a documentation style, select the one you're most comfortable with. This style will be used for formatting the text of the paper, the in-text citations, and the reference page.

2. After your instructor corrects your first draft, rewrite the paper and turn in a final draft. This version is to be as perfect as possible.

Why is it important to know that there are three distinct formats used to cite references? Because these styles differ in the way references are cited and bibliographies are formatted. It is imperative that you inquire which documentation style your instructor prefers. In any given term, you might have an English paper where MLA is the required format, an American government paper requiring the APA style, and another assignment requiring the Chicago style. Ask your instructors whether they have a preference and follow their directions. If your instructor does not have a preference, select the style that you find easiest to work with.

As a college student, you should purchase a writing manual. Most contain chapters on all three of the documentation styles. Select a writing manual that gives you enough examples so you can easily follow the formatting guidelines.

Recommended Handbooks

Diana Hacker, *Pocket Style Manual: Updated with MLA's 1999 Guidelines.* 1999. 187 pages. New York: Bedford Books. ISBN 0312247524.

Gerald Schiffhorst and Donald Pharr. *The Short Handbook for Writers.* 1997. 414 pages. New York: McGraw-Hill. ISBN 0070577617.

For information on the Chicago style, see

John Grossman, *The Chicago Manual of Style: The Essential Guide for Writers, Editors and Publishers,* 14th ed. 1993. 921 pages. Chicago: University of Chicago Press. ISBN 0226203897.

COMPUTER APPLICATIONS

CITATION STYLES WEB SITES

This web site at Long Island University has information on all citation styles.

http://www.liunet.edu/cwp/library/workshop/citation

The following web site at the University of Iowa, called "Karla's Guide to Citation Styles," links the user to various web sites that address citation styles.

http://www.baliwick.lib.uiowa.edu/library/cite/html

Purdue University has an extensive online writing laboratory (OWL) web site. For information on the APA and MLA citation styles, go to

http://owl.english.purdue.edu/Files/33.html

C O M P U T E R   E X E R C I S E   8.5

CITATION STYLES

In this exercise, you will take the four articles you used in Exercise 8.2 and put each in proper bibliographic form (the way you would prepare the bibliography for your paper). To complete this exercise, you will visit the citation style web sites referred to in this chapter's computer box on "Citation Styles Web Sites." For each of the four articles, write the bibliographic information using the MLA style, the APA style, and the Chicago style. Remember to use these web sites, and pay careful attention to detail. Indicate which web site(s) you used in completing this exercise.

Reference 1

MLA form: _____

_____

APA form: _____

_____

Chicago form: _____

_____

Reference 2

MLA form: _____

_____

APA form: _____

_____

Chicago form: _____

_____

Reference 3

MLA form: _____

_____

APA form: _____

_____

Chicago form: _____

_____

Reference 4

MLA form: _____

_____

APA form: _____

_____

Chicago form: _____

_____

Plagiarism

Plagiarism—presenting the words or ideas of others without giving proper credit—is both unethical and illegal. When you put your name on a piece of writing, the reader assumes that you are responsible for the information, wording, and organization and that you will acknowledge the source of any fact or idea that is not your own.

A writer cannot copy direct quotations without using quotation marks and acknowledging the source. Paraphrasing material or using an original idea that is not properly introduced and documented is another common type of plagiarism. Sloppy note taking, in which the writer has not distinguished between his or her thoughts and those of the sources, is a frequent culprit. To avoid plagiarism, follow these guidelines:

1. Introduce every quotation and paraphrase by citing, in the text of your paper, the name of the source of the material used.
2. Place quotation marks around all directly quoted material.
3. Rewrite paraphrased material so that it is faithful to the original ideas; rearranging sentences is not enough.
4. Document all source material used.
5. Include on the Works Cited or References page every source referred to in your paper.

The penalties for plagiarism can be severe; it is a serious offense. A student who has been caught plagiarizing can expect, at the least, to receive no credit for the assignment, and at some schools, expulsion is mandated.

Source: G. Schiffhorst and D. Pharr, *The Short Handbook for Writers* (New York: McGraw-Hill, 1997), pages 262–263.

Using someone else's paper and submitting it as your own is considered plagiarism. Buying papers and having someone (paid or unpaid) write a paper for you are also considered acts of plagiarism. Many instructors are now using software that helps to identify plagiarized papers.

CHAPTER 9

Goals and Values

So you find yourself on a college campus now. Several questions may be crowding your mind: How did I get here? Do I really want to be here, or was it just something to do or a way to get out of the house? Did my family or friends "push" me here? "This is getting scary," some students think, because all of a sudden they're looking at the rest of their lives. Wow! Let's take a look at your process of arriving here and what is ahead at the conclusion of your academic degree.

Most people for the first 18–20 years of their lives have been trained to be conformists—that is, to evaluate themselves on the basis of what others think of them, what others think they should be doing, or where others think they should be going. Parents instill this attitude to protect their children from harm during their formative years and to give them a sense of pride in who they are—racially, ethnically, religiously, and politically. However, there comes a time when representing the perspective and values of your social group may conflict in some respect with your sense of who you are. It is during your college experience that this generally occurs, so now is the time to clarify who you are, who you want to be, and where you want to go.

WHAT ARE VALUES AND GOALS?

Values are standards by which we judge ourselves and others. They are also standards by which we set priorities; that is, we have learned or developed a hierarchy of values that governs our goal-seeking behavior. A **goal** is a desired outcome to be attained in the future. Goals are frequently observed in our choice of occupation or profession. As an example, let's say I have a goal of helping people get well. My value or motivation is altruistic and nurturing, and I therefore attach a high priority to obtaining a medical degree so that I may exercise my value. This means that other goals, such as beginning a family or travel, may have to be postponed—a process known as delayed gratification. In this way, our values and motives actually help us determine our goals and the priorities we assign to them.

Behavior as a Vehicle

Figure 9.1 Values and motives in action

Our behaviors are the vehicles that put our values in action and carry us to our goals (see Figure 9.1).

Identifying Your Values

You have been in the process of developing your individual values ever since you were a child. The Personal Values Inventory® (PVI™) gives you the chance to explore your own values—both when things are going well for you and when you are faced with conflict or opposition. The PVI is based on Relationship Awareness® Theory, which was formulated by Elias H. Porter, Ph.D.

This theory has four simple yet powerful premises:

Premise 1. We all do what we do because we want to feel good about ourselves.

Premise 2. We tend to take two different approaches to life: one approach when we feel that things are going well, and another when we feel that we are faced with conflict or opposition.

Premise 3. A personal weakness is nothing more or less than the overdoing or the misapplying of a personal strength.

Premise 4. Our own motivational values influence the way we perceive the behavior of others.

The Personal Values Inventory (PVI) presents you with 20 items, each with three choices. The first 10 items are to be answered as you would when "things are going well," and the final 10 are to be answered as you would when "things are not going well." Each statement has three possible responses, which correspond to the three apexes on the PVI triangle (see Figure 9.2). The answers you provide are then scored and plotted on the scale on the triangle. This indicates in which portion of the triangle your "plots" intersect. Once you have plotted all of your scores, you connect them with a line that is interpreted to represent how the style you use to attain your goals and values differs depending on whether you believe things are going well or are not going well. It is interesting that some people find that others notice these changes before they themselves do. This may cause conflict, as you will see when we discuss relationships later in the chapter. If you are interested in taking the PVI or in obtaining more information, visit the web site for *The Transfer Student's Guide to the College Experience* at **http://college.hmco.com/students**.

UNDERSTANDING RELATIONSHIPS

Most models of human behavior are limited to observable behavior. They presume that by observing consistencies in a person's behavior patterns, it is possible to identify the person's characteristic traits of behavior or temperament and, from these traits, to predict the person's behavior accurately. Relationship Awareness Theory is a more complete, purposive (or motivational) model; it holds that behaviors are simply tools that people use to reach valued goals. Knowledge of a person's goals—what the person values—provides very important and accurate insight into the person's behavior and clarifies why he or she might act one way at one time and another way at another time.

The PVI identifies seven groups of values and motivations that can help you to understand and manage your relationships. Later in the chapter, we will explore how values and motives change when you feel conflict. People tend to be attracted to and stay in jobs where their motives and values are rewarded, yet anyone can excel in any environment. It's the purpose and desired results of the behavior that hold the key, not the behavior all by itself. People can be very happy doing things that they don't particularly care for as long as they can see the result they want in the end. Perhaps you don't like everything about college, but you continue because you want to achieve something important to you: a degree, financial security, acceptance by peers, a career, prestige, independence, or something else you value.

When people use behavior that doesn't make them feel good about themselves, but that represents an attempt to get a result that *would* make them feel good, Relationship Awareness Theory calls it "borrowing" a behavior.

A person's values and motivations fall into seven identifiable groups. We will demonstrate later how these appear to change, for the same person who is seeking a goal, between when things are going well for that person and when things are not going well.

We talk about "when things are going well" and "when things are not going well" when we plot the scores in the following example for Chris and Kelly. When the person who is seeking the goal construes her or his situation at that time as "things are going well," this is shown as the dot in Figure 9.2 for each person. When the individual seeking a goal values his or her situation in this quest as "things are not going well," this is shown by the arrowhead in Figure 9.2. The line connecting the two indicates how others see you change between when you perceive that things are going well for you and when you perceive that things are not going well for you in your goal-seeking behavior.

Refer to Figure 9.2 when reading this brief description of the clusters.

RED   =   Assertive–Directing
BLUE   =   Altruistic–Nurturing
GREEN   =   Analytic–Autonomizing
RED–BLUE   =   Assertive–Nurturing
RED–GREEN   =   Judicious–Competing
BLUE–GREEN   =   Cautious–Supporting
Circle (in the center =   Flexible–Cohering
of the triangle)

1. An Assertive–Directing cluster, a RED, refers to people who value the organization of people, money, and other resources in accomplishing their goals.
2. In the Altruistic–Nurturing cluster, a BLUE, we find people who value the protection and care of others.
3. People classified as GREEN, Analytic–Autonomizing, value thoughtful planning and want to ensure that, once begun, the steps or "rules" that define the way to achievement of goals are clear and straightforward.

Sometimes, however, an individual reflects a combination of these basic clusters.

4. With a RED–BLUE combination (Assertive–Nurturing), we find people who are assertive (RED) not for themselves but for the benefit of others (BLUE).
5. A RED–GREEN combination (Judicious–Competing) characterizes people who enjoy the competition (RED) of achieving their goals within the rules (GREEN).
6. A BLUE–GREEN combination (Cautious–Supporting) characterizes people who are thoughtful in developing a plan (GREEN) before moving ahead to use it to help others (BLUE).
7. A person who scores in the circle at the center of the PVI triangle, either when things are going well or when things are not going well, is called Flexible–Cohering. These individuals are the team players who will sacrifice personal goals for the sake of the group.

UNDERSTANDING MOTIVATION

When an ambulance drives aggressively—sirens blaring, lights flashing, running red lights, driving on the wrong side of the road—we understand it and accept it because we know the ambulance's purpose is to help someone. When we see a regular car driving aggressively like that, we may feel, say, or express

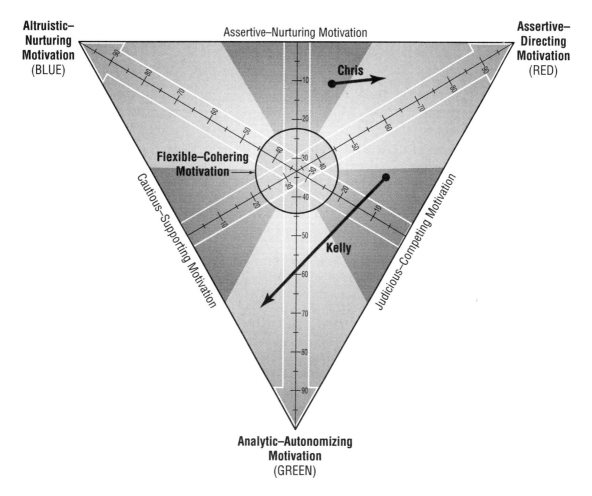

Figure 9.2
PVI results for Chris and Kelly

through a gesture something very different from understanding and acceptance. But if we knew that the driver of that car had a pregnant woman in labor as a passenger and was on the way to the hospital, we could understand the driving style and even approve of it.

The ambulance's driving style is like a person's behavior. Sometimes we may feel threatened by other peoples' behavior because we don't understand why they are behaving that way. If we understand that other people are doing things to feel good about themselves (the first premise of Relationship Awareness

Theory), we can think about how that behavior may be making them feel good about themselves and can approach them from that perspective. If you reflect on the times when other people have approached you and assumed that you were doing something good and compare that to the times when other people assumed you were trying to take something away from them or hurt them in some way, you will see the power of this simple idea.

Refer to Figure 9.2. Chris's PVI results are in the Red–Blue (Assertive–Nurturing) part of the triangle when things are going well and in the Red part of the triangle during conflict. Kelly's PVI results are in the Red–Green (Judicious–Competing) part of the triangle when things are going well and in the Green part during conflict. When things are going well, it is likely that Chris and Kelly will agree—both will want to get things done quickly, will be willing to take risks, and will be alert to opportunities. Yet they may have some different values around people or processes. Chris is likely to want to take action for the benefit of others, and Kelly is more likely to pursue a strategic objective. These motives and values shape the two individuals' perceptions and judgments about each other's actions. Over time, we might hear Kelly describe Chris as a pushover—too worried about other people's needs and not focused on the bottom line. Chris, on the other hand, may describe Kelly as unfeeling—so focused on the bottom line that other people get hurt in the process (or by the process). Each perceives the other person as overdoing a strength to the point where it becomes a weakness. When these perceptions of overdone strengths persist, interpersonal conflict can result.

Managing Conflict

Relationship Awareness Theory recognizes that motives change when people are in conflict. The whole purpose of conflict is to defend what's important to us so we can get back to doing the things that make us feel good about ourselves again. If we can't defend our values successfully, we may change motives again and go deeper into the conflict, perhaps feeling a bit more uncomfortable too. As we progress through the three stages of conflict (see Figure 9.3), our focus narrows, and all the energy of conflict is concentrated in that narrower focus. If you have ever said something like "Well, just forget about them. What I want out of this is . . ." that may have been a time that you went from stage 1 of conflict to stage 2. Stage 2 is when the other person tends to drop out of focus.

If you were to complete the PVI, your arrow would probably not be exactly like anyone else's in your class. Some people's PVI results end up drawing an arrow whose beginning (dot) is very close to the end (arrowhead), and others have those points very far away from each other. The distance reflects how much change there is in the individual's values and motives between when things are going well and when conflict begins. If the dot is close to the arrowhead, the change is probably very small and is not noticeable at first. If the dot

The Stages of Conflict	Areas of Focus
Stage 1	Maintaining self-worth *Focus on self, problem, and other*
Stage 2	Preserving self-worth *Focus on self and problem*
Stage 3	Protecting self-worth *Focus on self*

Figure 9.3
The hierarchy of the preservation of self-worth

is far from the arrowhead, the change is large and is probably obvious to other people.

Refer to Chris and Kelly from Figure 9.2. If Chris and Kelly were in a car and were having a problem (say that they realize they are running late to a very important event and aren't exactly sure how to get there), what would happen? It's likely that Chris (who is Red first in conflict) would see this as a challenge and want to drive a little faster or go a little farther to see whether the next intersection would be the right one. Kelly (who is Green first in conflict) is more likely to be cautious and to consult the map or use logic. Because of the differences in their initial responses to conflict, they are likely to view each other's behavior as inappropriate. For example, Kelly could see Chris as taking unnecessary risk, gambling that the next intersection would be the right one. These perceptions often lead to the conflict getting worse.

How, then, can conflict be avoided? And is that even the right question? There are lots of conflicts that should happen. Imagine how boring the world would be if everyone agreed on everything. Perhaps we should be asking ourselves how to recognize conflict and manage it most effectively. Because when conflict is about defending what's important, conflict can actually help us to learn what's important to ourselves and to other people. When we see people using their conflict behavior, we can remember that they are trying to get back to their other behavior—the patterns they exhibit when things are going well again. If we can find a way for their conflict behavior to "work" without putting us into conflict, we can resolve the conflict. Thus Kelly could suggest that Chris keep driving while Kelly reads the map, or Chris could ask Kelly to read the map while Chris drives. Whoever recognizes the conflict first can take the lead in finding a way for the conflict behavior to work and get everyone feeling good about the situation again.

Sometimes though, you could experience a conflict all by yourself. You might care about two things but only be able to do one, or choosing one thing might automatically exclude something else that you value.

Value/Goal Conflicts

In Exercise 9.1 you will be asked to identify some of your goals and values and to rate them with a score from 1 (least important) to 10 (most important). After you have identified and rated your values and goals, we will try to determine what happens when they conflict.

Let's consider someone whose PVI result is in the Green when things are going well and who has two potentially conflicting values or goals, "support my family" and "become a college graduate." It's easy to see how these two things could conflict: Supporting a family often involves working steadily, which takes time away from school. If supporting the family is given a rating of 10 on the scale and graduating is given a rating of 7, we might expect that this person would drop out of college someday if the family needs were great enough. A future conflict like this could be managed by coming to an understanding with family members that the best way to support them in the long run is to make a few sacrifices now in pursuit of the college degree. This is not easy, and your conflicts are probably not easy either. But it still makes sense to plan ahead so that you will know what to do when conflict happens.

When our values or goals conflict, we are faced with a choice and must answer some tricky questions.

- Which goal or value has the highest priority?
- Which one will hurt others the least or help others the most?
- Can these values or goals be reconciled in such a way as to attain both at the lowest cost?

How do we make such choices? Parents and family have taught us to make decisions in terms of values consistent with our race, ethnicity, religion, gender, or even political heritage. You may choose to alter, modify, or abandon any of these decision-making guidelines when you are independent, but initially, this process was intended to ensure our earliest "teachers" that when we were away from them, the familial values would still shape our decision-making.

Why Did You Transfer?

Exercise 9.2 asks you to identify at least one major goal you have regarding your transfer to this university. This exercise can be used in conjunction with your regular visit to your academic advisor either to assess your progress or to

E X E R C I S E 9.1

VALUE/GOAL CONFLICTS

The purpose of this exercise is to help you examine value/goal conflicts that may occur, so that you can be prepared to manage them.

1. In the first column in the table, identify your goals or values. Some items to consider for your list are family, children, job/occupation success, being my own boss, spirituality, my significant other, my country, my race or ethnic group, my sense of personal power, and graduating from college.

2. After you have identified your own values or goals, briefly explain why each of them is important to you and give it a rating, or score, from 1 (least important) to 10 (most important). How is each of your values or goals related to your PVI results?

3. For each of the values or goals, write down the other values or goals that it could conflict with—and how you could manage that conflict.

Value or Goal	Rating	Why It's Important	Potential Conflicts	Conflict Management Strategies

E X E R C I S E 9.2

HOW AM I DOING?

In the column at the top left, write your goal. For the remaining column headings, write in some time periods, such as years, semesters, or terms.

In the leftmost column, write in the way you will measure progress toward your goal. If your goal is to graduate by a certain date, how will you know whether you are making good progress? Such measures might include your grade point average (GPA), the number of required courses you have completed, the number of theme courses completed toward your major or minor, and the number of general education courses completed. You may wish to expand the table to include additional measures or a longer time frame.

Example:

Goal: Graduate with honors	1st quarter	2nd quarter	3rd quarter
Measure: G.P.A.	Plan: 4.0 Actual: 2.8	Plan: 4.0 Actual: 2.97	Plan: 4.0 Actual: 3.2

Goal:	1st _____	2nd _____	3rd _____
Measure:	Plan: Actual:	Plan: Actual:	Plan: Actual:
Measure:	Plan: Actual:	Plan: Actual:	Plan: Actual:
Measure:	Plan: Actual:	Plan: Actual:	Plan: Actual:
Measure:	Plan: Actual:	Plan: Actual:	Plan: Actual:

In this manner you can monitor your own progress by the measures you and/or the university have set. This is particularly crucial if you decide to change majors or to add a minor to your academic program.

revise your goals in accordance with the information and experience you have gained since your transfer.

THE IMPORTANCE OF RELATIONSHIPS

You've often heard it said: "It's not what you know; it's who you know." Who do you know? Think about your important relationships, and as you identify people, write their names on the graph shown in Figure 9.4. Write their names higher up in the graph if they are able to help you achieve your goals. Write their names more to the right on the graph if you spend a lot of time with them. If you spend the most time with the person who can help you the most, that name would be in the top right corner of the graph. It is also helpful to think in what part of the PVI triangle each person's scores would be located.

Temperament

Finally, proceed to Exercise 9.3 and, utilizing the web site for the Keirsey Temperament Sorter, answer the questions. This computer-based analysis will also help you reflect on what you know about yourself.

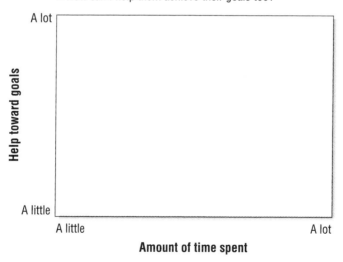

Figure 9.4
Personal contacts who are assets in my goal-seeking

COMPUTER EXERCISE 9.3

KEIRSEY TEMPERAMENT SORTER

Log on to the Internet. Then go to **http://www.keirsey.com** and take the Keirsey Temperament Sorter (from *Please Understand Me* and *Please Understand Me II* by David Keirsey).

1. In what ways were the results from this instrument similar to those of the inventory you completed in Exercise 9.1? How were they different?

_____

_____

_____

_____

_____

2. If the results are not similar, how would you explain this?

_____

_____

_____

_____

_____

3. Discuss your findings with another member of the class to compare the information you have found.

Why Did We Do This?

The purpose of these exercises is to help you to clarify the values that motivate your actions and to understand that they are the basis for what you have chosen as goals, both in your personal life and in your professional life.

CHAPTER 10

Careers and Majors

They want me to declare a major! What do I do? There are a lot of things I'd like to do, but none of them is in the catalog!

First, don't worry about making a mistake or being unable to state what career you will have for the next 40 years. People change jobs, specific work assignments, or careers an average of every 4–5 years and even more frequently in some industries. And in the last half of the 20th century, people changed careers, on average, four times in the typical 40-year work span. Therefore, your task is not to lay out a specific plan for the rest of your life but to select a major in a general area of interest.

How are careers and majors related? Well, in some industries there is no relationship between a specific major and a career. Examples include police officers and sales representatives. For some fields, however, such as communications, architecture, nursing, engineering, or music, you should major in that discipline because the occupation is so specific. In still other areas, such as business administration, medicine, and law, the technical training is so specific that it can be gained only in graduate school.

There are a number of career counseling offices and job placement centers to which we shall refer you later. But initially, the most significant concern for the future is your present.

FUTURE WORK RELATIONSHIPS

One way to begin thinking about careers or professions in which you might function smoothly is to list and describe the types of relationships that you find productive and enjoyable. You will be spending a lot of time with your co-workers, so it is important that your tasks—and especially your relationships—be comfortable. In such a setting, you will be more likely to achieve both interpersonal satisfaction and a sense of accomplishment in your career.

EXERCISE 10.1

FUTURE WORK RELATIONSHIPS

In this exercise, you are to list the types of interpersonal relationships with which you feel most comfortable when accomplishing tasks. For example, you might respond, "I like to work as part of a team" or "I prefer to work by myself and report the results when I'm finished." What sorts of interpersonal relationships do you envision as most enhancing your productivity and enjoyment on the job?

_____

_____

_____

_____

_____

_____

_____

_____

_____

_____

_____

Another way to locate your career interests, both known and unknown, is to find a similarity between what you currently find interesting and how these interests correlate with those of persons who are already working in various occupations/jobs. In Exercise 10.2, you are to visit the web site of the United States Department of the Interior. This site has a large array of self-administered self-assessment and exploration surveys to help you establish an occupational focus.

PREPARING TO ENTER THE WORK FORCE

Exercises 10.3 through 10.6 prepare you for the workplace with mock interviews at an actual firm, Procter & Gamble, and then by having you develop a résumé first for a hypothetical person and later for yourself. These exercises are designed to stimulate your recollection of the abundant experiences and skills you have acquired to date at part-time jobs, in your classroom course assign-

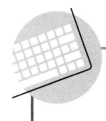

COMPUTER EXERCISE 10.2

U.S. DEPARTMENT OF THE INTERIOR CAREER MANAGER

Visit this U.S. Government web site, **http://www.doi.gov/octc/**, and list below all of the web site addresses that assist you in your career or occupation search and what each offers for you.

_____

_____

_____

_____

_____

_____

_____

_____

Now compare this information with what you learned in Exercise 10.1. This comparison should assist you in narrowing down to a shorter list your field of occupational or career interest(s).

ments, during extracurricular activities, and even in discharging responsibilities at home.

Now that you have found that all or nearly all of your life experiences can be described in terms appealing to a prospective employer, rate them from 1 to 10 (that is, from lowest to highest) on your feeling of your competence in these areas. Keep this as a worksheet for future applications you will make.

Examine the summary of qualifications and letter of application for a sales associate position in Figure 10.1 and Figure 10.2. The applicant is currently a student and has been working at a McDonald's fast-food restaurant. The application is to Nordstrom's, an upscale department store. It illustrates reflecting on one's current or previous job experience to explain to a prospective employer the job skills one currently possesses.

Note that Exercise 10.5 requires you and your small-group discussion section to develop a summary-of-qualifications résumé for two persons. In Exercise 10.6, you will prepare for *yourself* a résumé based on your life experiences and education to date.

E X E R C I S E 10.3

MOCK INTERVIEW WITH PROCTER & GAMBLE

Another device that can assist you in your decision making is the mock interview. In this exercise, we will use the actual questions given to people who apply for a job with the Procter & Gamble Corporation.

Describe a situation where you have demonstrated the following. (This is at any point in your life to date.)

1. Leadership skills _____

_____

_____

2. Communication skills _____

_____

_____

3. Creativity and innovation _____

_____

_____

4. Initiative and follow-through _____

_____

_____

5. Priority setting _____

_____

_____

6. Problem solving _____

_____

_____

7. Goal achievement _____

_____

_____

After you have made your written notes, the instructor will ask one student to act as the interviewer while you act as the prospective employee. Present in oral form the answers you have prepared for the seven points in the foregoing Procter & Gamble interview.

Then write answers to the following questions and be prepared to discuss them.

1. What did thinking about and presenting these remarks do for your self-knowledge of your experiences to date?

_____

_____

_____

_____

_____

_____

_____

_____

2. What did you feel was left out or did not fall into a category covered in the assigned questions?

_____

_____

_____

_____

_____

_____

_____

_____

LOCATING THAT FIRST JOB

As you begin (usually during your senior year) to accumulate lists of organizations, companies, or positions to fit with your academic degree and personal goals, you should summarize that information. Exercise 10.7 will help you in that process.

EXERCISE 10.4

RÉSUMÉ WRITING

This exercise requires you to reflect on your past work experiences from middle school through the present. The purpose is to help you recognize and define the experience and skills you have already attained. In this process you will gain insight into the preparation of future résumés for employers. These résumés will be based on the "summary-of-qualifications" format, rather than on the chronological listing of employers and job titles. Record the transferable skills you have attained from each of the following to date:

Chores at home (such as organizing your mowing of the yard into blocks of time for efficiency)

_____

_____

_____

_____

Course work at school (such as the observation study you had to conduct off campus, or the chemistry experiment you had to devise)

_____

_____

_____

_____

Extracurricular activities (such as the Meals on Wheels program for which you volunteered and became dispatcher of other drivers)

_____

_____

_____

_____

Your current part-time job (such as the responsibility to serve customers directly, operate an electronic cash register, maintain counter inventory, and ensure hygiene of the sales area)

_____

_____

_____

_____

Jose Barreras
1515 Anywhere Street
Los Angeles, CA 90063

POSITION DESIRED: Sales Associate

SUMMARY OF QUALIFICATIONS:

- Over four years experience in daily retail sales for major fast-food chain;

- Experienced in working in multicultural environment of both fellow workers and customers;

- Accomplished at multi-sale point cashier operations;

- Experienced at inventory management and control;

- Experienced in maintaining high standards of cleanliness and order in department.

EXPERIENCE:

1996 to present	Assistant shift manager, McDonald's, 22200 Olympic Blvd., Culver City, CA 90009
1994–1996	Retail sales, McDonald's, 22200 Olympic Blvd., Culver City, CA 90009

EDUCATION:

1994–present	Student, California State University, Los Angeles, Marketing major
1994	Graduate, Roosevelt High School

REFERENCES: available upon request.

Figure 10.1—Example of a summary-of-qualifications résumé

Jose Barreras
1515 Anywhere Street
Los Angeles, CA 90063

December 4, 1998

Ms. Joyce Santo Diamond
Human Resources Department
Nordstrom's Corporation
3333 Corporate Drive
Montebello, CA 91754

RE: Job Application

Dear Ms. Santo Diamond:

I have enclosed my résumé for the position of sales associate at Nordstrom's. I am
applying for this position for two reasons:

      [1] I have always respected the Nordstom customer policy of helpfulness
           and courtesy to all customers, exhibited by your sales associates,
           which makes the working environment pleasant for all concerned;

      [2] I have the experience in multicultural retail sales and customer
           relations which, I believe, can be an asset to your corporation.

I hope to schedule an appointment with you in the near future.

Thank you for your consideration.

Yours truly,

Jose Barreras
Enclosure: Summary of Qualifications

Figure 10.2—Example of an application letter

EXERCISE 10.5

WRITE TWO RÉSUMÉS

Your small-group discussion section should now write a résumé for each of the following people, who are applying for a management trainee position.

PERSON A

Worked at In and Out Burger for six years (every step of the process was learned) from food processing to customer service; ran cash register and drive-thru window.

Progressed to assistant manager.

Does volunteer work at the local Boys Club supervising/advising/mentoring 12- to 16-year olds.

Graduated from Schurr High School in 1992 with a B– average. [Be sure to say *graduated from,* not just *graduated.*]

Took part in soccer, tennis, gymnastics, and wrestling.

PERSON B

Worked at Wendy's for six years (focused on final prep of food orders, cash register, and drive-thru service).

Progressed to shift leader.

Graduated from Schurr High School in 1992 with a C+ average.

Played football, volleyball, and basketball.

Works as a Police Volunteer on weekends.

Interpretation

Finally, each group should write its résumés on the chalkboard, and the groups should discuss which résumé for each applicant is most effective and why.

Having completed these résumés, you will be better prepared to assess your own skills and interests and communicate them in a summary-of-qualifications résumé for yourself.

First you will list all of the people with whom you have developed relationships in your academic field while in college: teachers, laboratory assistants, other students, and other professionals. Add to this list the search mechanisms made available by your academic discipline and always available at the annual national or regional meetings that you should have been attending. List the

E X E R C I S E 10.6

YOUR RÉSUMÉ

It is time for you to write a summary-of-qualifications résumé to communicate your current basis of experience, both academic and otherwise, to any prospective employer.

At your next class meeting, share your résumé with another group and have them evaluate it for completeness and effectiveness. On the basis of what they read, would they hire you?

various services provided by the Career Counseling Office on your campus and, last but not least, the World Wide Web sites available. Exercise caution with web sites, particularly if they want money to help you. You must investigate them thoroughly through the Better Business Bureau and your state's consumer affairs office before enlisting any aid from them.

However, not everyone goes directly from a four-year university into the work force. Some occupations require advanced postgraduate academic work.

GRADUATE AND PROFESSIONAL SCHOOLS

Because of the interests you have recently discovered, many of you will find that completing a four-year degree program is only the beginning of your career development. You may decide to apply to graduate school.

What Do Graduate Schools Look for in Applicants?

Each graduate program is unique. To ascertain its specific requirements, you need to write or email its graduate admissions department. Also, be sure to contact the department in which you would pursue your intended graduate degree for similar information.

In general, you begin your trek to a graduate degree with your high school performance, because this is what established the level of your entry into the university (as a regularly admitted student, a special admit, or other category). Special admission is *not* a deterrent to acceptance into a graduate program, but it does underscore the significance of your academic performance at the four-year university.

You might look at admission to a graduate program as a series of hurdles on a track field.

Hurdle 1 is your undergraduate grade point average. Most graduate programs expect a 3.2 or higher in the 4-point system in order to consider an applicant. However, this is not an absolute, and hurdle 2 is generally of greater significance.

E X E R C I S E   10.7

COMPILING DATA FOR YOUR JOB SEARCH

Organize this segment in any manner that helps you make decisions. If area of the country is important, then begin your first subdivision with that; if type of industry is important, then being with that; and so on.

MY PROFESSIONAL NETWORK
Organize these entries in terms of how much you think they would be able to help, judging on the basis of their current and past work experiences and how well you know them. Do not forget to include relatives.

Name	Address(es)	My Relationship

CONTACTS THROUGH MY DISCIPLINE (from conferences, etc.)
Again, organize by the degree to which these people might be able to assist you in obtaining useful job/career information.

Name	Address(es)	Organization

CAMPUS COUNSELING SERVICE

List all of the various services that this office can provide. Contact the counseling service at least six months before graduation. Set up an appointment with a counselor and find out what this office can do for you now and in the future. List these services below.

Person Contacted	Telephone Number/email	Services for me

DEPARTMENTAL CHAIR/ADVISOR

Always speak with this person about his or her knowledge of the discipline, the work world, and even his or her network of colleagues in academe and elsewhere.

Professor	Telephone Number/email	Advice/names

Hurdle 2 is the Graduate Record Examination (GRE), which tests reading comprehension, verbal analogies, and quantitative skills. Again, each school will have its own "threshold" score for consideration, but this, too, is not absolute. Hurdle 3 is also significant.

Hurdle 3 consists of the letters of reference from faculty who can attest to your academic ability and, more important, to your potential as a graduate student.

Hurdle 4 is evidence of your extracurricular activities and/or leadership from high school through the present. This is significant because it is a measure of your ability to communicate and relate to the larger community.

After you have cleared these four hurdles, the last measure is your personal interview at the university of your choice.

The interview consists of several parts. The first and most formal part is meeting with the faculty responsible for such interviews—with one or more of the senior faculty who will be determining where you will fit into their program (perhaps as a research assistant or a teaching assistant). This is when the personal statement that you included in your application becomes critical. You must incorporate elements of your life experiences. In many instances, these seemingly unrelated life experiences may affect whether you are accepted even more than your GRE scores or letters of reference. There is another, rarely discussed but significant, aspect of your interview: Informal as it is, it will reflect your "social capital"—that is, your ability to represent this graduate institution in a positive manner in social situations. Your appearance and demeanor should illustrate that you know how to dress, speak, and behave appropriately in social settings. Therefore, before your on-campus interview, review a book of manners or etiquette. It can't hurt, and it might make all the difference.

Preparing for the On-Site Campus Interview for Graduate School

After you have received all of the information you requested via email or regular post, always check the web site of your prospective campus and department. Check the list of faculty in the department and through the abstract listings in every major library, locate their recent professional publications, and read at least the abstracts of their articles or reviews of their books. In this way, you can speak knowledgeably to specific faculty members, not in terms of substantive issues, but of their work—particularly if it is in your area of interest and this might be the person with whom you would prefer to work. Also, be prepared to visit with and listen to current graduate students on that campus for hints about the workload and other matters of interest.

We have now presented you with several different ways to zero in on a field of study for your undergraduate degree and have suggested how to assess your interests and skills, how to evaluate your current level of experiential expertise, and how to prepare for either a job interview or entrance into a graduate program. You have also compiled a wide array of information about your prospective field of endeavor. And you have learned how to prepare an eye-opening summary-of-qualifications list for your résumé. GO FORTH AND MAKE YOUR CONTRIBUTION TO THE WORLD!

CHAPTER 11

Money Management

Did you know that one of the most common causes of stress in the general population is financial pressure? You, as a college student, are probably just as stressed out about money as are other adults. In addition, you are probably in debt. Research finds that most college students graduate with debt. There are two general sources of debt: college loans and credit cards. The goal of this chapter is to give you tools to minimize the amount of debt you incur while in college by suggesting ways to manage your money more effectively.

Now, if your parents are paying for everything, this chapter won't be important to you right now. But save this book anyway. As soon as you graduate from college and have to start paying your own way, you'll find the information in this chapter useful.

TAKING CONTROL

Many of us let money control us instead of controlling our money. The first step in gaining control over your finances is understanding how much you spend and how you spend it (otherwise known as keeping a budget). We all have a general idea of where our money goes, but taking a closer and more systematic look at your spending habits can provide you with important information on ways to save money.

Personal Spending

The worksheet in Exercise 11.1 is organized into three general sections related to your monthly spending: Net Income (how much you have each month to spend), Variable Expenses (expenses that vary from month to month), and Fixed Expenses (payments that must be made each month). Complete this form as accurately as possible.

Variable Expenses

For these expenses, you need to estimate the average amount spent each month for each category. For example, if you get your hair cut and styled once every two months and it costs $30.00 each time, the cost per month is $15.00. Don't forget to include large, one-time expenses, such as vacations and weekend get-aways. Calculate how much you spend each year on trips, and divide that amount by 12 to get a monthly average. And yes, the $3.00 you spend on your twice-weekly double cappuccino does count as a dining expense. Even the microwave popcorn from the vending machine counts as a food expenditure (the nutritional value of the meal has no bearing on whether it qualifies as a food expense).

Fixed Expenses

As the name suggests, fixed expenses do not fluctuate from month to month. Therefore, they are easier to calculate than variable expenses. Examples of fixed expenses are car payments and rent. You know exactly how much you will have to budget for these items.

Reducing Spending: Easier Said Than Done!

No one likes to reduce spending. It hurts! Often, spending money makes us feel good. Buying a new CD or a new sweater brings you pleasure. You enjoy listening to music, and wearing that new sweater makes you feel good about yourself. There is no denying the powerful positive feelings associated with buying things. Likewise, going to the coffeehouse every day for a cup is enjoyable. You can sit and relax and meet friends, and it tastes great. That experience is something you can't readily duplicate at home.

The trouble with overspending is that you ultimately pay the price for this extravagance—both financially and psychologically. The short-term price is increased anxiety and stress. This is something college students already have in ample supply, and you don't need any more. Some students start working more hours to pay their bills, delaying their graduation date while adding expense upon expense. We have even known students who turned down their dream job because their personal debt was so high that they had to take a job that paid more just so that they could pay all their bills.

In serious cases, overspending can ruin your financial credit. In the not so distant future, bad credit could make it very difficult, if not impossible, for you to purchase important things such as a home, furniture, or a car on credit. Or you could become one of the high-risk loan candidates who can get credit only by paying outrageous interest rates. It can take seven to ten years of excellent credit to overcome a bad credit record.

The initial step in trying to reduce spending is to keep a daily log of how you spend your money. Many times, it's the little things we don't pay attention to that start to add up to a big black hole in the budget. Buying lunch on campus

E X E R C I S E 11.1

PERSONAL BUDGET WORKSHEET

Part One. Monthly Net Income

Net wages (after taxes) .... $_____

Grants, scholarships, loans .... $_____

Other income (allowances, etc.) .... $_____

TOTAL MONTHLY INCOME $_____

Part Two. Monthly Variable Expenses

Food/beverages (supermarket shopping) .... $_____

Car (gas, maintenance, tires, repairs) .... $_____

Utilities (electricity, gas, water) .... $_____

Phone (local and long-distance) .... $_____

Cable TV/Internet services .... $_____

Laundry, dry cleaning .... $_____

Clothing purchases .... $_____

Medical/dental/prescriptions .... $_____

Hair care, beauty treatments .... $_____

Entertainment (dining, movies, concerts, CDs, hobbies) .... $_____

Vacations (spring break, winter vacation) .... $_____

Books, supplies, newspapers, magazines .... $_____

Gifts, dues, contributions .... $_____

Miscellaneous .... $_____

TOTAL VARIABLE EXPENSES $_____

Part Three. Monthly Fixed Expenses

Rent, mortgage, room .... $_____

Tuition .... $_____

Car payment .... $_____

Car insurance .... $_____

Student parking fees .... $_____

Credit card payments .... $_____

Health insurance .... $_____

Life insurance	$_____
Homeowners/renters insurance	$_____
Other fixed expenses (child care, etc.)	$_____
Contribution to savings	$_____
TOTAL FIXED EXPENSES	$_____

TOTAL INCOME	$_____
minus TOTAL VARIABLE EXPENSES	−$_____
minus TOTAL FIXED EXPENSES	−$_____
DIFFERENCE	$_____

If the difference is positive, congratulations! You're one of the very wise adults who are living within their means. If you have a negative difference, however, you have to reduce spending in one or more of the categories.

or purchasing a coffee and sweet roll for breakfast isn't an outrageous individual expenditure. But the cumulative effect on your spending can be significant. Say you spend $5.00 per day on either breakfast or lunch, and you do this 5 times during the week. It's only $5.00 per day, but it's $25.00 per week and $100 per month. Over the course of a year, that's approximately $1200! And over 4 years, it's $4800 (not including tips).

This is why the first step in evaluating your personal spending habits is to keep an accurate and honest log of every penny you spend. Exercise 11.2 will help you keep track of every expenditure for a week.

Motivations for Spending

People spend money for various reasons, many of which are psychologically based. If someone is insecure, buying an expensive sports car might be an effort to improve that person's self-image. Of course, we all know that advertisers would never suggest that driving this type of car will make you feel powerful, fun, and sexy. Yeah, sure we do! The subtle message communicated is that if you buy this car, the lifestyle associated with it (powerful, fun, and sexy) will be yours too. The reality is that you are getting an expensive, high-maintenance car with outrageous insurance premiums. Not only won't you automatically be powerful, fun, or sexy, but you probably won't even be able to afford to date! (The commercial never shows the new car owner agonizing each month when it is time to write a check for a very substantial car payment.)

For others, spending is a way to buy friendship. The (perhaps subconscious) idea is that when you pay for others, they will like you and be your friend. Treating a friend on occasion is a wonderful and generous act and a sign of a

E X E R C I S E 11.2

PERSONAL SPENDING LOG

For seven consecutive days, record every penny you spend. You must include *everything:* snacks, coffee, soft drinks, copy machine, video games, haircut, movie tickets, etc. (But exclude major bills, such as rent, utilities, insurance, and car payments.) This particular log will reveal how much you're spending on personal items and activities. Draw your personal Spending Log on a separate sheet of paper, using the format suggested below. You will turn in this log with your assignment. *Hint:* It's a good idea to carry your Log in your wallet to make it easier for you to record your spending for the week.

SPENDING LOG

Date	Item	Amount	Date	Item	Amount

After you keep track of your personal spending for seven consecutive days, read over your expenditures carefully and consider the following questions.

1. How would you describe your personal spending habits? Do you overspend or underspend? If so, by how much—a lot, moderate amounts, or just a little? In what ways and in what categories of spending do you over- or underspend?

_____

_____

_____

2. List those items or activities where you tend to overspend or spend unnecessarily. *Example:* buying lunch because you didn't have time to pack a meal to take to school.

_____

_____

_____

3. What influenced you to overspend or spend unnecessarily?

_____

_____

_____

4. What items and/or activities could you have survived without? What items and/or activities have a less expensive alternative? *Example:* Instead of going to the movies for $15.00 (ticket, popcorn, drink) you could have rented a video for less than $5.00 (rental, microwave popcorn, drink).

_____

_____

_____

5. Pick at least one item or activity that you will no longer spend money on. How much will you save on a daily, weekly, monthly, and annual basis? How difficult will it be not to purchase this item or engage in this activity any longer? Can you substitute a lower-cost alternative?

_____

_____

_____

6. Pick at least one item that you will reduce spending on. *Example:* Reduce going out to dinner from six times a month to three times a month. How much will this save you each month?

_____

_____

_____

thoughtful human being. However, paying frequently is the act of an insecure person who is being taken advantage of by his or her so-called friends.

It is important to get a better understanding of the type of relationship you have with money. Do you use money to buy love, to wield power, or to comfort yourself? When you become aware of your personal motivations for spending, you become able to exert more control over your spending patterns. Remember that the goal is not to stop spending and become a hermit but to control your money, rather than having your money control you.

EXERCISE 11.3

MONEY MOTIVATIONS

Answer each of the following questions. Then score your answers to help pinpoint the meaning of money for you and what motivates you to spend it. (Test from "Personal Money Motivation," by the Consumer Credit Counseling Service of Los Angeles.)

1.____ Money is important because it allows me to:
   a. do what I want to do
   b. feel secure
   c. buy things for others
   d. show people that I am important

2.____ I feel that money:
   a. frees up my time
   b. can solve my problems
   c. is a means to an end
   d. helps make relationships smooth

3.____ When it comes to saving money, I:
   a. don't have a plan and don't often save
   b. have a plan and stick to it
   c. don't have a plan but manage to save anyway
   d. don't make enough money to save

4.____ If someone asks about my personal finances, I:
   a. feel defensive
   b. realize I need more education and information
   c. feel comfortable and competent
   d. ask friends or family first

5.____ When I make a major purchase, I:
   a. go with what my intuition tells me
   b. research a great deal before buying
   c. feel I'm in charge—it's my (our) money
   d. ask friends or family first

6.____ If I have money left over at the end of the month, I:
   a. go out and have a good time
   b. put the money into savings
   c. look for a good investment
   d. buy a gift for someone

7.____ If I discover I paid more for something than a friend did, I:
   a. couldn't care less
   b. feel it's okay because I also find bargains at times
   c. assume he or she spent more time shopping, and time is money
   d. feel upset and angry at myself

8.____ When paying bills, I:
   a. put it off and sometimes forget
   b. pay them when due, but no sooner
   c. pay when I get to it but don't want to be hassled
   d. worry that my credit will suffer if I miss a payment

9.____ When it comes to borrowing money, I:
   a. simply won't—I don't like to feel indebted
   b. only borrow as a last resort
   c. tend to borrow from banks or other lending institutions
   d. ask friends and family because they know I'll pay

10.____ When eating out with friends, I prefer to:
   a. divide the bill proportionately
   b. ask for separate checks
   c. charge the bill to my bank card and have others pay me
   d. pay the entire bill because I like to treat my friends

11.____ When indecisive about a purchase, I often tell myself:
   a. it's only money
   b. it's a bargain
   c. it's a good investment
   d. he or she will love it

12.____ In my family:
   a. I handle all the money and pay all the bills
   b. my parents (partner) take care of all the finances
   c. I pay my bills and my parents (partner) pay theirs (his or hers)
   d. My parents (partner) and I sit down and pay the bills together

To calculate your score and identify your personal money type:

Count the number of a's, b's, c's, and d's.

If you have a majority of a's, you are a free spender. You get a kick out of spending money freely, without regret.

If you have a majority of b's, you value safety and enjoy security with money.

If c's are the majority of your answers, you enjoy the power of money. It's an ego booster, and you want things you can't afford.

Finally, if you have a majority of d's, you have a tendency to use your money to buy love.

CREDIT CARDS: TAMING THE BEAST

Today's society is becoming increasingly cashless; in other words, we use credit cards more often than we use cash. This is not necessarily a bad thing, but you, as a consumer, need to understand the advantages, disadvantages, and pitfalls associated with relying on credit cards. Like many things in life, credit cards can be useful or harmful, depending on how they are used.

Establishing Credit

It is important that you start to establish credit in your own name. How do you do this? One of the easiest ways is to apply for a credit card. Local credit cards with local businesses and department stores or a local bank or credit union are a good way to start. These cards usually have lower issuance standards than the major credit card lenders. Gasoline credit cards also are fairly easy to obtain. The best strategy is to get a card, make a few very small charges, and pay your balance in full. By doing this, you will have established a credit history. If you so desire, you can then do some research and find a low-interest major credit card (such as Visa, MasterCard, or Discover). If you obtain a major credit card, it should be used for emergencies only. And as one financial expert has remarked, if you can wear it or eat it, it isn't an emergency! *Hint:* At this stage avoid department store cards. They tempt you to spend unnecessarily and they are usually limited to just one chain of stores.

You need to be aware that major credit card companies target college campuses, hoping to sign up college students with offers of free T-shirts, water bottles, phone calling cards, and other incentives. Unfortunately, many students who sign up for these credit cards later find themselves in serious financial trouble. In the past few years, over 300 colleges and universities have banned credit card marketers from their campuses. It is estimated that another 150 universities are in the process of adopting similar policies.

Student Debt: A National Problem

According to Nellie Mae (the nickname of an institution that provides student loans), the average undergraduate has nearly $2000 in credit card debt. A recent study by the Consumer Federation of America and sociologist Robert Manning suggests that 20% of students at four-year universities carry credit card debt of $10,000 or more (that is not a misprint). The following chart indicates how long it takes, and what it costs in interest payments, to pay off varying amounts of credit card debt. Remember, these numbers assume that no additional charges are made to the credit card while you are paying off the debt.

Debt: $2,000 (average credit card debt of college students); *Interest Rate:* 18% APR (the national average for college students)

	Repayment Period				
	1 yr	2 yr	3 yr	4 yr	5 yr
Payments	$183/mo	$100/mo	$72/mo	$59/mo	$51/mo
Total Interest	$200	$396	$603	$820	$1047

Thus, if you pay about $50.00 per month on your $2000 credit card debt, and if you don't make any more charges to the card, it will take you 5 years to pay off the debt, and the $2000 will actually cost you $3047 because of the interest charged. Unfortunately, that example was the good news regarding credit card debt. Here's the bad news: Those students with $10,000 in credit card debt will have to pay $180 per month for 10 years in order to pay off that balance. And they will have paid $11,622 in interest charges. The interest will exceed the original $10,000 charge. And if you can't afford $180 per month in repayment and pay only $150 each month, it will take you 30 years to pay off the debt. The interest alone, paid over 30 years, is a whopping $44,250!

School administrators and credit counselors have reported cases where students reduced their course load in order to work more hours just to keep up with their credit card payments. As Lonnie Williams, director of a consumer-counseling center in Austin, Texas, reports,

> We see some students reduce course load to work more hours at a part-time job. We also see them apply for student loans to pay off what they've run up on credit cards. In some cases they drop out for a semester or a year and think they can pay it all off and go back. Once they've left school, it gets real hard to go back.

What this all means is that it pays (literally and figuratively) to learn how to handle credit carefully and intelligently. Your future livelihood depends on it. Renting an apartment, getting hired for a job, and applying for a home mortgage or a car loan all require a good, clean credit record. The following ten steps, offered by Lisa Lazarony of Bankrate.com, can help you handle credit wisely:

1. Always remember that credit is a loan. It's real money that you must repay. Before you apply for the first card, decide what the card will be used for—emergencies only? school supplies?—and determine how the monthly bills will be paid.
2. Go slowly. Get one card with a low limit and use it responsibly before you even consider getting another.
3. Shop around for the best deal.
4. Study your card agreement closely, and always read the fine-print flyers enclosed with every bill. Credit card offers differ substantially, and the issuer usually can change the terms at will with 15 days' notice.

Courting students

Tina Fanetti, 24, a graduate student at Iowa State University in Ames, Iowa, got her first credit card in her freshman year. Soon, 11 other issuers rushed to give the jobless student more than $12,000 in credit lines. She fell behind in her payments, got charged late fees, endured penalty rates of 21.9 percent, exhausted her savings, borrowed from one card to make payments on another, took out student loans to pay the credit cards, and saw her credit rating ruined before she entered her adult life. Her advice to other students enticed by credit card come-ons: "Don't. The biggest mistake I ever made was getting credit cards. I never believed—until now—that the credit-card companies wouldn't think twice about skinning me alive." (From "New Assault on Your Credit Rating," *Consumer Reports,* January 2001, p. 22.)

Bob Daemmrich/Stock Boston

5. Try to pay off your total balance each month. Just paying the minimum is a trap: If you pay off a $1000 debt on an 18% card by just sending in the minimum each month, it will take more than 12 *years* to repay.

6. Always pay on time. A single slip-up will place a black mark on your credit record—and is likely to cause your issuer to jack up your interest rate to the maximum.

7. Set a budget, follow it closely, and watch how much you're paying on credit. A good rule of thumb is to keep your debt payments less than 10% of your net income after taxes. So if you take home $750 a month, spend no more than $75 a month on credit.

8. Keep in touch with your issuer by notifying the company promptly when you move. In the event that you must be late on a payment, call them before it's late. They want your business for life, so they may be willing to make arrangements that won't leave a mark on your credit rating.

9. Close all accounts you aren't using. Having available-but-unused credit counts against you when it comes time to buy a car. That's because lenders don't like it when you have the ability to go deep into debt quickly.

10. At the first sign of credit danger, such as using one card to pay off another, make the card more difficult to use. Carry it only when you plan to use it, lock it up in an inaccessible place, or entrust it to your parents.

COMPUTER EXERCISE 11.4

CREDIT CARDS

1. How many credit cards, if any, do you have in your name?

_____

2. List each card (do not list account numbers) and the balance you currently have on each card.

_____

_____

_____

_____

_____

3. For each card that has a balance, go to the web site **http://www.bankrate.com**. At that web site, click on the top tab "calculators." On the Calculators page, find the section "Credit Card Calculators" and click on the line "Calculate the real cost of your debt." Figure 11.1 will appear on your screen.

Calculate The
REAL COST
Of Your Debt

How much is my loan costing me?

Loan amount	
Years to pay off loan	
Interest rate (%)	
Monthly payment	
Total interest	

Figure 11.1
The real cost of your debt

Source: Bankrate.com. Republished with permission; permission conveyed through Copyright Clearance Center, Inc.

You will need to supply the information requested. Type in the credit card balance (the amount you owe on your card) in the "Loan amount" space. Type the number 1 in the "Years to pay off loan" space. And then type in the interest rate you're currently being charged on that specific card (the current interest rate is printed on your monthly credit card statement). The amount of your monthly payment and how much interest you will be charged will automatically appear in the box. This information reflects how much you will have to pay each month for a 1-year period of time to pay off the current balance.

4. Use the credit card calculator to determine your monthly payments and the total interest you will pay if you pay off your credit card in 1 year, 2 years, and 5 years. Do this for every credit card for which there is a current balance. List all the information for 1-, 2-, and 5-year payoff periods for each card.

_____

_____

_____

_____

5. What is the total of the credit card monthly payments you would need to make to pay off all of your cards in 1 year? In 2 years? In 5 years? To answer this question, you will need to complete Question 4 and then add up the monthly payments for all of your cards if you were to pay off your debts in a 1-year period. Do the same for 2-year and 5-year periods.

_____

_____

_____

_____

6. Can you afford the monthly payments to clear your balances in 1 year? Why or why not? How long will it take you to pay off your credit card debts? Remember that these calculations are based on the assumption that you will make no new charges to your existing accounts.

_____

_____

_____

_____

PROTECTING YOUR CREDIT: IDENTITY THEFT

Identity theft is one of the fastest-growing crimes. In identity theft, someone gets ahold of some vital information of yours, poses as you, is able to get into your bank and/or credit card accounts, and rips off the money. You are left holding the bag. One of this book's authors was recently victimized in this way (it was not fun). This unfortunate experience could ruin your credit rating and take a lot of your time and effort to undo the damage inflicted on you. Given all the other challenges you face, you don't need this additional pressure.

Here are some ways to help prevent identity theft:

- Carefully guard documents with important personal information. Papers containing your bank account and PIN numbers, credit card information, social security number, birth certificate, and any other type of identity information should always be kept in a safe and secure place. Never keep account numbers and PIN numbers on the same piece of paper or close to each other.

- Do not give out your social security number unless absolutely necessary. Your social security number is often used to gain access to important financial accounts. Someone who manages to obtain your social security number could pose as you and gain access to your money. They can also use your number to obtain credit cards and loans. Do not think that just because you have few assets, people who obtain your social security number present little threat to your financial security. They can fraudulently obtain loans and/or credit cards in your name and ruin your credit rating for years. You don't need money in the present for these thieves to hurt you. They steal your future.

- Do not leave outgoing mail in your mailbox for the mail carrier to pick up. Thieves look for mail awaiting pickup, knowing that there are often checks in the envelope. In fact, the only safe place to mail bills is inside the Post Office. It is not even completely safe to use the outside mailboxes on the Post Office premises.

- Do not leave credit card slips or bank ATM receipts in public places. These little slips of paper have important account information printed on them. The same goes for self-service gas stations when you use a credit card and the machine prints out a receipt.

- Never give personal information to anyone over the phone, no matter how nice they seem or how innocent they sound. These people are good at pretending to be something they are not. Ask them to send you their request for information in writing.

- When providing sensitive information over the Internet, make sure the web site is secured and legitimate. (Some would argue that there is no way to be completely sure of this.)

FINANCIAL AID

By this point in your college experience, you probably have a lot of information on the types of financial aid available to you. Your campus financial aid office is a great place to visit for an update on what types of loans, grants, scholarships, and work-study programs are currently available. There also are excellent web sites that provide a wealth of information about college financial aid. Three of the best sites are

FastWeb at **www.fastweb.com**

Project EASI at **www.easi.ed.gov**

FinAid! The Smart Student Guide to Financial Aid at **www.finaid.org**

Make periodic checks of financial aid available online. Your circumstances may have changed, or new sources may become available. Don't let sources of money pass you by because you didn't find them on your initial search.

A visit to your campus employment office could also be beneficial. On- and off-campus employment opportunities are usually posted there. Also keep an eye open for professors seeking students to work on research projects.

Graduate and Professional Education Costs

If you plan to go to graduate or professional school after receiving your Bachelor's Degree, you will need to find ways of funding those additional years of education. Graduate and professional schools usually are quite expensive, especially if you are paying out-of-state tuition at a public university. The good news is that, depending on your area of study, you may be offered a fellowship, scholarship, or assistantship. Unlike much undergraduate financial aid, graduate awards are based on merit (scholarship), not financial need. These financial packages usually pay your tuition and provide you with a monthly stipend for living expenses. In return, the institution may want you to be a research assistant or teaching assistant. Such reciprocal work plans often are not required when one is awarded a scholarship or fellowship.

Professional schools, such as medical or dental programs and law schools, are not as likely to make these programs available. Although some scholarships are available, these financial packages are usually extended only to highly accomplished students whom the institutions try to lure to their programs by offering them paid tuition and other benefits.

For many, going on to professional and graduate study requires securing loans. Again, a visit to your institution's financial aid office will be helpful, as will requesting financial aid information from prospective graduate and professional schools. This is another good reason to control your spending efficiently as an undergraduate.

E X E R C I S E 11.5

FINANCIAL AID/SCHOLARSHIP OFFICE

Locate and visit your institution's financial aid and/or scholarship office. Be prepared to ask specific questions related to your personal situation (credit card debt, graduate school loans, work-study program, etc.). After your visit, answer the following questions.

1. What specific information did you hope to get at your financial aid/scholarship office?

_____

_____

_____

2. What did you find?

_____

_____

_____

3. In what ways was your visit helpful or not helpful?

_____

_____

_____

4. What, if any, additional steps will you be taking to improve your financial situation?

_____

_____

_____